The Riches of Intercultural Communication

# Utrecht Studies in Language and Communication

*Series Editors*

Paul van den Hoven
Jan D. ten Thije

VOLUME 38

The titles published in this series are listed at *brill.com/uslc*

# The Riches of Intercultural Communication

*Multilingual and Intercultural Competences Approaches*

VOLUME 2

*By*

Roselinde Supheert
Gandolfo Cascio
Jan D. ten Thije

BRILL

LEIDEN | BOSTON

Cover illustration: detail from *A Woman Standing at an Open Sash Window, a Small Boy beside Her* by Anthonie Andriessen. The Metropolitan Museum of Art, New York (public domain).

Library of Congress Cataloging-in-Publication Data

Names: Supheert, R., author. | Cascio, Gandolfo, author. | Thije, Jan D. ten, author.
Title: The riches of intercultural communication : multilingual and intercultural competences approaches / by Roselinde Supheert, Gandolfo Cascio, Jan D. ten Thije.
Description: Boston : Brill, [2022] | Series: Utrecht studies in language and communication, 0927-7706 ; volume 38 / series editors, Paul van den Hoven, Jan ten Thije | Includes bibliographical references and index. | Contents: v. 38 : v. 2 : pt. 4 Multilingual Approach – v. 38 : v. 2 : pt. 5 Transfer / Intercultural Competence Approach.
Identifiers: LCCN 2022038994 (print) | LCCN 2022038995 (ebook) | ISBN 9789004522480 (v. 38, v. 2 ; Hardback : acid-free paper) | ISBN 9789004522855 (v. 38, v. 2 ; eBook)
Subjects: LCSH: Intercultural communication. | Communication and culture.
Classification: LCC GN345.6 .S863 2022 (print) | LCC GN345.6 (ebook) | DDC 303.48/2–dc23/eng/20220929
LC record available at https://lccn.loc.gov/2022038994
LC ebook record available at https://lccn.loc.gov/2022038995

Typeface for the Latin, Greek, and Cyrillic scripts: "Brill". See and download: brill.com/brill-typeface.

ISSN 0927-7706
ISBN 978-90-04-52248-0 (hardback)
ISBN 978-90-04-52285-5 (e-book)

Copyright 2023 by Roselinde Supheert, Gandolfo Cascio, and Jan D. ten Thije. Published by Koninklijke Brill NV, Leiden, The Netherlands.
Koninklijke Brill NV incorporates the imprints Brill, Brill Nijhoff, Brill Hotei, Brill Schöningh, Brill Fink, Brill mentis, Vandenhoeck & Ruprecht, Böhlau, V&R unipress and Wageningen Academic.
Koninklijke Brill NV reserves the right to protect this publication against unauthorized use. Requests for re-use and/or translations must be addressed to Koninklijke Brill NV via brill.com or copyright.com.

This book is printed on acid-free paper and produced in a sustainable manner.

# Contents

List of Figures and Tables   VII
Notes on Contributors   IX

### PART 4
*Multilingual Approach*

11  Speaking Dutch in Indonesia: Language and Identity   3
    *Martin Everaert, Anne-France Pinget and Dorien Theuns*

12  The Effect of Migration on Identity: Sociolinguistic Research in a Plurilingual Setting   28
    *Elisa Candido*

13  The Impact of Bilingual Education on Written Language Development of Turkish-German Students' L2   42
    *Esin Işil Gülbeyaz*

14  Linguistic Advantages of Bilingualism: The Acquisition of Dutch Pronominal Gender   59
    *Elena Tribushinina and Pim Mak*

### PART 5
*Transfer / Intercultural Competence Approach*

15  Different Frames of Reference [The Thing about Dutch Windows]   79
    *Debbie Cole*

16  Education, Mobility and Higher Education: Fostering Mutual Knowledge through Peer Feedback   93
    *Emmanuelle Le Pichon-Vorstman and Michèle Ammouche-Kremers*

17  English & Cultural Diversity: A Website for Teaching English as a World Language   111
    *Bridget van de Grootevheen*

18  Intercultural Ethnographies of Students Abroad: International Experience Becomes Intercultural Learning   124
   *Jana Untiedt and Annelies Messelink*

19  The Intercultural Deskpad: A Reflection Tool to Enhance Intercultural Competences   141
   *Karen Schoutsen, Rosanne Severs and Jan D. ten Thije*

Appendix: Contents Volume 1   161
Index of Names   163
General Index   164

# Figures and Tables

### Figures

| | | |
|---|---|---|
| 12.1 | Geographic spread of Albanian dialects | 29 |
| 12.2 | Participant auto valuation of the four skills | 31 |
| 12.3 | Years of residence in Italy by group | 35 |
| 13.1 | Maas' model of language enhancement: orate to literatre continuum | 44 |
| 13.2 | Category grid for syntactic analysis of written language development in Turkish and German | 52 |
| 14.1 | Percentage of masculine pronouns, by group | 66 |
| 19.1 | Three phases of the *Intercultural Deskpad* | 155 |

### Tables

| | | |
|---|---|---|
| 11.1 | Excerpt 1 | 11 |
| 11.2 | Excerpt 2 | 11 |
| 11.3 | Excerpt 3 | 12 |
| 11.4 | Excerpt 4 | 12 |
| 11.5 | Excerpt 5 | 13 |
| 11.6 | Excerpt 6 | 13 |
| 11.7 | Excerpt 7 | 13 |
| 11.8 | Excerpt 8 | 14 |
| 11.9 | Excerpt 9 | 14 |
| 11.10 | Excerpt 10 | 15 |
| 11.11 | Excerpt 11 | 15 |
| 11.12 | Excerpt 12 | 15 |
| 11.13 | Excerpt 13 | 16 |
| 11.14 | Excerpt 14 | 17 |
| 11.15 | Excerpt 15 | 17 |
| 11.16 | Excerpt 16 | 17 |
| 11.17 | Excerpt 17 | 18 |
| 11.18 | Excerpt 18 | 18 |
| 11.19 | Excerpt 19 | 20 |
| 11.20 | Excerpt 20 | 21 |
| 11.21 | Excerpt 21 | 22 |
| 11.22 | Excerpt 22 | 23 |
| 11.23 | Excerpt 23 | 24 |

| | | |
|---|---|---|
| 14.1 | Coefficients of the comparisons between groups | 66 |
| 17.1 | Assignments in the second iteration, including order of difficulty and logical order | 117 |
| 18.1 | Overview of modules of pilot course "Intercultural Training" | 126 |
| 18.2 | Overview of frequency of all 690 text parts that represented learning phases | 130 |
| 19.1 | Overview of training activities linked to learning outcomes and intercultural competences | 151 |

# Notes on Contributors

*Michèle Ammouche-Kremers*
is assistant professor of French Literature and Culture at Utrecht University and University College Utrecht. She manages the Language Assistant Program of Utrecht University.

*Elisa Candido*
is lecturer of Communication and Information Studies at Utrecht University. Her fields of expertise are sociolinguistics, pragmatics and intercultural comunication. She published "Vivere il plurilinguismo. La comunità albanofona nel comune di Maniago," in *Ad Limina Alpum. VI Colloquium Retoromanistich, Cormòns 2–4 Otubar 2014*, ed. Frederico Vicario (Udine: Società Filologica Friulana, 2016): 77–96.

*Gandolfo Cascio*
is assistant professor of Italian Literature and Translation Studies at Utrecht University. His areas of research are reception aesthetics and digital philology. He has published the monographs *Michelangelo in Parnaso. La ricezione delle «Rime» tra gli scrittori* (Venice: Marsilio, 2019; English trans. Leiden: Brill, 2022). *Dolci detti. Dante, la letteratura e i poeti* (Venice: Marsilio, 2021; Nino Martoglio Prize) and the collection of essays *Le ore del meriggio. Saggi critici* (Castiglione di Sicilia: Il Convivio, 2020; G.A. Borgese Prize). Currently he is carrying out the ICON-funded project Observatory on Dante Studies.

*Debbie Cole*
is associate professor of Linguistic Anthropology at Utrecht University. She published "The Emergent Selectivity of Signs and the Projection of Protopersonae," in *Contact Talk: The Discursive Organization of Contact and Boundaries*, eds. Zane Goebel, Debbie Cole, and Howard Manns (New York: Routledge, 2020); *The element of Surprise—A Play in One Act*, in *Urban Utopias: Memory, Rights and Speculation*, eds. Barnita Bagchi and Sujaan Mukherjee (Kolkata: Jadavpur University Press, 2020); and authored "Looking for Rapport in the Metacommunicative Features of an Ethnographic Interview," in *Rapport and the Discursive Co-construction of Social Relations in Fieldwork Encounters*, ed. Zane Goebel (Berlin: De Gruyter, 2019): 17–31.

*Martin Everaert*
is emeritus professor of Linguistics at Utrecht University. He mainly publishes on the syntax-lexicon interface, language evolution, and language variation.

His latest publications are (with Bernadette Kushartanti and Hans van de Velde) "Acquiring Social and Linguistic Competence: A Study on Morphological Variation in Jakarta Indonesian Preschoolers' speech," in *Sociolinguistic Variation and Language Acquisition across the Lifespan*, eds. Anna Ghimenton, Aurélie Nardy, and Jean-Pierre Chevrot (Amsterdam: John Benjamins, 2021): 104–128; with Henk van Riemsdijk he edited *The Wiley-Blackwell Companion to Syntax I–VIII* (Hoboken: Wiley-Blackwell, 2017; 2nd edition); and wrote (with Martinus Huybregts and Noam Chomsky et al.) "Structures, Not Strings: Linguistics as Part of the Cognitive Sciences," *Trends in Cognitive Sciences* 19, no. 12 (2015): 729–743.

*Bridget van de Grootevheen*
has been an affiliated researcher to Utrecht University. Her fields of expertise are education and intercultural communication.

*Esin Işıl Gülbeyaz*
is lecturer at the department of Languages, Literature and Communication of Utrecht University and is an expert on Multilingualism. Her recent publications include "Syntaktische Komplexität bei Satzverknüpfungsverfahren mehrsprachiger SchülerInnen in ihrer Erst- und Zweitsprache," in Isabel Fuchs, Stefan Jeuk, and Werner Knapp, eds., *Mehrsprachigkeit: Spracherwerb, Unterrichtsprozesse, Schulentwicklung Beiträge zum 11. Workshop Kinder und Jugendliche mit Migrationshintergrund* (Fillibach bei Klett: 2017): 111–134; *Schriftspracherwerb und Mehrsprachigkeit. Syntaktische Komplexität bei Satzverknüpfungsverfahren mehrsprachiger Schülerinnen und Schüler in ihrer Erst- und Zweitsprache* (Munster: Waxmann, 2020); "Correlation between Language Biographies and Written Language Development of Bilingual Students in Their L1 and L2, Taking into Account the Nature and Extent of First Language Instruction in a Bilingual vs. Monolingual Setting," in Erwin Gierlinger and Marion Döll, eds., *Teaching Subject-Specific Content in a Plurilingual Classroom* (Münster: Waxmann, forthcoming).

*Michèle Ammouche-Kremers*
is assistant professor of French Literature and Culture at Utrecht University and University College Utrecht. She manages the Language Assistant Program of Utrecht University.

*Emmanuelle Le Pichon-Vorstman*
is assistant professor at the University of Toronto, OISE, head of the Centre de Recherches en Éducation Franco-Ontarienne (CRÉFO). Her research focusses

on issues related to multilingual education. Since 2009, she has led several projects on the inclusion of minority students in education. Her latest publications are (with Jim Cummins and Jacob Vorstman) "Using a Web-based Multilingual Platform to Support Elementary Refugee Students in Mathematics," *Journal of Multilingual and Multicultural Development* (2021): 1–17; (with Nathalie Auger) *Défis et Richesses des Classes Multilingues: Construire des Ponts Entre les Cultures* [Challenges and opportunities of multilingual classrooms: Building bridges between cultures] (coll. "Pédagogies" ESF Sciences Humaines, 2021); with G. Prasad and Nathalie Auger she edited *Multilingualism and Education: Researchers' Pathways and Perspectives* (Cambridge: Cambridge University Press, in press).

### Pim Mak

is assistant professor of Language and Communication at Utrecht University. His areas of expertise include language processing and first and second language acquisition. His publications include (with W. Vonk and H. Schriefers) "Discourse Structure and Relative Clause Processing," *Memory & Cognition* 36, no. 1 (2008): 170–181; (with Gerda Blees) "Comprehension of Disaster Pictorials across Cultures," *Journal of Multilingual and Multicultural Development* 33, no. 7 (2012): 699–716; (with Julia Lomako, Natalie Gagarina, Ekaterina Abrosova and Elena Tribushinina) "Keeping Two languages apart: Connective Processing in Both Languages of Russian-German Bilinguals," *Bilingualism: Language and Cognition* 23, no. 3 (2020): 532–541.

### Annelies Messelink

is strategic policy advisor at the Rotterdam Business School. She has recently published (with Jan Van Maele) "Intercultural Foreign Language Teaching and Learning in Higher Education Contexts," in *Mobilizing Essentialist Frameworks in Non-Essentialist Intercultural Training*, 141–161, Information Science Reference, 2019; (with Jan D ten Thije) "Unity in Super-Diversity: European Capacity and Intercultural Inquisitiveness of the Erasmus Generation 2.0." *Dutch Journal of Applied Linguistics* 1, no. 1 (2012): 80–101; and (with Jan Van Maele and Helen Spencer-Oatey) "Intercultural Competencies: What Students in Study and Placement Mobility Should Be Learning," *Intercultural Education* 26, no. 1 (2015): 62–72, DOI: https://10.1080/14675986.2015.993555

### Anne-France Pinget

is assistant professor at the department of Language, Literature and Communication of Utrecht University and researcher at the Fryske Akademy (Leeuwarden, the Netherlands). Her research spans three domains: sociolinguistics (sound change, imitation, language attitudes), sociophonetics, and second language acquisition (acquisition of variation, language policy, fluency, accent, attitudes). She authored with Hans Rutger Bosker, Hugo Quené, and Nivja de Jong "Native Speakers' Perceptions of Fluency and Accent in L2 Speech," in *Language Testing* 31, no. 3 (2014): 349–365; (with René Kager and Hans van de Velde) "Linking Variation in Perception and Production in Sound Change: Evidence from Dutch Obstruent Devoicing," *Language and Speech* 63, no. 3, (2020): 660–685; "First Language Effects on the Identification and Evaluation of Second Language Speech: The Case of Second Language Dutch as Spoken by Francophone Learners," *Nederlandse taalkunde* 26, no. 2 (2021): 171–194.

*Karen Schoutsen*
is trainer and coordinator of trainings on intercultural competences for employees at Utrecht University, as well as coordinator careers orientation at the department of Languages, Literature and Communication of Utrecht University. Her field of expertise is intercultural competences and multilingualism. She published (with Ineke van den Berg, Stefan Südhoff, and Jan D. ten Thije) "Luistertaal in het Hoger Onderwijs," *Neerlandia: Nederlands-Vlaams Tijdschrift voor Taal, Cultuur en Maatschappij* 120, no. 4 (2016): 34–35; (with Jan D. ten Thije and Emmy Gulikers) "Het Gebruik van Luistertaal in de Praktijk. Een Onderzoek naar Meertaligheid in de Bouw, de Gezondheidszorg en het Onderwijs in Nederland en Vlaanderen" [https://taalunie.org/publicaties/118/het-gebruik-van-luistertaal-in-de-praktijk] 2020.

*Rosanne Severs*
is founder and managing director of Globi, center of expertise for internationalization in education. Her special field of interest is intercultural competence development of students and educational professionals. She is involved in course development and training for Utrecht University staff.

*Roselinde Supheert*
is an assistant professor of English Language and Literature at Utrecht University. Her research focuses on adaptation, reception and intercultural communication. Recent publications include (with Roos Beerkens, Emmanuelle Le Pichon-Vorstman, and Jan D. ten Thije, eds.) *Enhancing Intercultural Communication in Organizations: Insights from Project Advisers* (Routledge Focus on Communication Studies. New York, NY: Routledge, 2020); and the *Map Your Hero(ine)* website: https://mapyourhero.com/

*Dorien Theuns*
is an independent visual anthropologist and community programmer at the Stedelijk Museum Schiedam. Together with Martin Everaert she developed the website *Indo in Indonesië:* https://www.indo-in-indonesie.com/

*Jan D. ten Thije*
is professor emeritus of Intercultural Communication at the Department of Languages, Literature and Communication at Utrecht University. His main fields of research concern institutional discourse in multicultural and international settings, receptive multilingualism, intercultural training, language education, and functional pragmatics. From 2007 to 2021 he coordinated the Master's program in Intercultural Communication at Utrecht University. He is connected to the Institute for Language Studies, Department of Languages, Literature and Communication at Utrecht University. Previously he was also connected to Chemnitz University of Technology and University of Vienna. He has been engaged in intercultural and multilingual counselling and training activities in urban, academic, and European Committee constellations. Publications include (with Roos Beerkens, Emmanuelle Le Pichon-Vorstman, and Roselinde Supheert, eds.) *Enhancing Intercultural Communication in Organizations: Insights from Project Advisers* (Routledge Focus on Communication Studies. New York, NY: Routledge, 2020); (with Ludger Zeevaert) *Receptive Multilingualism: Linguistic Analyses, Language Policies, and Didactic Concepts: Hamburg Studies* on Multilingualism (Amsterdam: John Benjamins, 2007). He is editor in chief of the *European Journal for Applied Linguistics* (EuJAL) published by Mouton de Gruyter and Series editor of *Utrecht Studies in Language and Communication* (USLC) published by Brill Publications, Leiden.

*Elena Tribushinina*
is associate professor of English Linguistics at Utrecht University. Her areas of expertise cover first and second language acquisition, child bilingualism, developmental language disorders and foreign language pedagogy. Her recent publications include (with Elena Dubinkina-Elgart, Nadezhda Rabkina) "Can Children with DLD Acquire a Second Language in a Foreign-language Classroom? Effects of Age and Cross-language Relationships," *Journal of Communication Disorders* 88 (2020); (with Zoë op ten Berg and Sonja Karman) "Facilitating Positive L1 Transfer through Explicit Spelling Instruction for EFL Learners with Dyslexia: An Intervention Study," *Language Awareness* (2021); (with Mila Irmawati and Pim Mak) "Macrostructure in the Narratives of Indonesian-Dutch Bilinguals: Relation to Age and Exposure," in *Linguistic Approaches to Bilingualism* (2021).

*Jana Untiedt*
has left academia to work as a researcher in the corporate world, studying and understanding human behavior in international multinationals.

# PART 4

## *Multilingual Approach*

CHAPTER 11

# Speaking Dutch in Indonesia: Language and Identity

*Martin Everaert, Anne-France Pinget and Dorien Theuns*

## 1        Introduction[1]

This paper deals with Dutch spoken in Indonesia. That is, Dutch spoken by Indonesian state citizens who acquired Dutch at a very early age, in a period in which Dutch was an official language in Indonesia, so basically before 1945, and Indonesia was a colony of the Netherlands: the Dutch East Indies (*Nederlands-Indië*). The speakers are elderly (70+ years old) and linguistically quite diverse. Some could be called simultaneous bilinguals, living in a bilingual environment from birth, speaking Dutch at home, and Indonesian or indigenous languages like Javanese, Sundanese, or Madurese in everyday life (cf. also De Vries 1976). Others are early bilinguals, who learned Dutch at a young age at primary school. Most of the speakers, but not exclusively so, are of Eurasian descent. What makes this group special is the fact that they can only speak Dutch in certain contexts. Speaking Dutch constitutes and reflects, to some extent, a part of their identity. It is this aspect that we will focus on in this study. Besides examining the larger social, historical and political context in which Dutch was spoken in Indonesia, this study, situated in the field of linguistic anthropology, draws on personal interviews conducted in Indonesia with around 50 speakers. The aim is to examine these speakers' language use, language practices and language ideologies and show how they constitute and reflect their identity (see also Bucholtz and Holt 2004). In section 2 we will sketch the speech community and its speakers. Section 3 gives a brief description of the status of Dutch in the colonial period, and the transitional phase during the Second World War

---

1  Martin Everaert & Anne-France Pinget: Utrecht University; Dorien Theuns: independent visual anthropologist/programmer City Museum Schiedam. We owe a lot to discussions with, and help of, Jan-Karel Kwisthout, Hans van de Velde, Ulbe Bosma, Jurriaan Koning, Kiki Kushartanti, Emma Everaert. We would like to acknowledge very helpful comments from the editors. Readers who understand Dutch are also invited to visit the website www.indo-in-indonesie.com. This research was made possible with support from the Instituut voor de Nederlandse Taal and Utrecht University.

and the period immediately after the war when Indonesian became the official state language. Section 4 illustrates how speaking Dutch for this group constitutes part of their identity.

## 2  The Population of the Dutch East Indies

During the colonial period Dutch East Indies society was characterized by huge socio-economic differences, racial inequality, political oppression and class differences, as in many other colonies. From a purely judicial perspective society was divided into 'Europeans' (primarily, but not exclusively Dutch), the indigenous people (in colonial terms *inlanders*) and 'Foreign Orientals' (in colonial terms *vreemde oosterlingen*, which include Arabs and Chinese).[2] Each group had its own status, with associated rights and obligations. From a societal perspective, we could distinguish a fourth group: people of Eurasian descent, the 'Indo-Europeans' (*Indo-Europeanen*), also called *Indos*,[3,4] most of whom were classified as Europeans,[5] meaning they mainly held Dutch citizenship. For people of Eurasian descent their European status depended on whether they had a European father, either in marriage or acknowledged outside of marriage. There was also the option of applying for the status of European, with constantly changing conditions. In the colonial period this was called *gelijkstelling* ('being made equal to'), an option also available to Indonesians, Chinese, etc.[6]

In the 20th century Indos who held the European status began to define themselves along ethnic, racial and legal lines (Meijer 2004). In 1919 the Indo-European Union (*Indo-Europeesch Verbond*, IEV) was established for and by Indo-Europeans. The IEV was an emancipation movement that fought for

---

[2] This threeway division was introduced by law in 1920.
[3] The *Woordenboek der Nederlandse Taal* (the equivalent of the OED for the Dutch language) has no entry for *Indo-Europeaan* and a very short entry for *Indo*: "als benaming voor iemand van gemengd Indisch (inlandsch) en Europeesch bloed in Ned. Oost-Indië" [as a name for someone of mixed Indonesian (native) and European blood in the Dutch East Indies].
[4] When we use the word 'Indo-European' we refer to Dutch *Indo-Europeaan*, to be distinguished from Dutch *Indo-Europees*, as the name of a language family.
[5] For most scholars Indo-Europeans were Europeans by definition. For instance, Van der Veur (1990, 113) gives the following definition. "Indo-Europeans are persons of mixed blood, with a European ancestor, who were considered 'Europeans' in the East Indies colonial society." However, there were also people of mixed European-Asian descent not legally recognized as Europeans. A number of our interviewees belong to the latter group.
[6] To give you an idea on how often this happened, Beets et al. (2002) mention that in the period 1920–1941 approximately 11,000 people received European status.

equality and political control and influenced all areas of social life. By 1930, the IEV had nearly 15,000 members. They strove for an independent nation that would remain connected to the Netherlands, but with an important position for Indos. In practice, the IEV stood up for the interests of the middle class Indo (Bosma and Raben 2008). It should be noted here that in this period Indo-Europeans/Indos in the legal sense did not exist. Being Indo-European had no legal meaning; you were either European, or not (Bosma, Raben and Willems 2006).[7] Dutch colonial law never attributed a separate legal status to Indo-Europeans like, for example, the *Métis* in the French colonies or the *Eurasians* and *Anglo-Indians* of the Raj (Anderson 2011). Indos never appeared as a category in colonial censuses, but it is probable that they made up to two-thirds of the 240,000[8] 'Europeans' recorded by the census of 1930. Precise figures on the number of people of Eurasian descent who lacked Dutch citizenship are not available. To give some idea of the size of the groups mentioned, the Resistance Museum Amsterdam[9] (based on Beets et al. 2002) gives the following numbers: 60,000 'white' Dutch; 200,000 Dutch Indo-Europeans; 1,200,000 Chinese; 60,000,000 Indonesians.

The word *Indo* has carried different meanings and connotations in different periods. In the colonial period, the meaning was basically 'of Eurasian descent,' a racial classification, but in the 20th century it was very much a matter of class (Bosma, Raben and Willems 2006). It had a clear negative connotation in the Japanese and revolution period. Nowadays for many Dutch Indos, but not all, the word does not have a negative connotation. For some it even has a positive meaning (of identity). We use the term because almost all of the people interviewed used the term to refer to themselves; our interviewees identified themselves as Indo,[10] or *Indische mensen* (Indies people).[11]

Indos quite often had the status of 'Europeans' and would thus have, in principle, access to facilities that were only accessible for Europeans. This was not the case for those of Eurasian descent who did not have this status; they

---

[7] With one exception: during the Japanese occupation your ethnicity played a role. White Europeans were always incarcerated, Indo's in principle not, but there were many exceptions.
[8] Based on Beets et al. (2002).
[9] https://www.verzetsmuseum.org/en/kennisbank/the-pre-war-dutch-east-indies.
[10] Giving a complete overview of the different interpretations of the word *Indo* over time and in different contexts lies beyond the scope of this article (cf de la Croix 2013).
[11] 'Indisch' refers to the Dutch East Indies, and often includes white Dutch living in the colonies for a longer period, and Indo's. (cf. Beets et al. 2002 on how this term is used in the Netherlands).

often lived in poverty. The European Indos worked primarily as civil servants, in education, services, the Royal Netherlands East Indies Army (*het Koninklijk Nederlandsch-Indisch Leger*, KNIL). Although by law there was no distinction between white Europeans (*totoks*) and European Indos, this distinction was, of course, present in many ways in the social domain. Bosma, Raben and Willems (2006), however, argue that in the colonial and post-colonial society in addition to their Eurasian descent, education, employment and income were the most important factors determining the place of Indos and other Europeans: "From the very beginning of Dutch colonialism, racial, legal, religious and class categories have been intermingled" (Bosma, Raben and Willems 2006, 147–148; our translation). In late colonial society, the concept of race became increasingly prominent, but the formal distinction was not as clearcut.

In summary, every citizen in the Dutch East Indies was a Dutch subject (*onderdaan*). But only a small group was a Dutch citizen (*staatsburger*), meaning that they possessed a Dutch passport, and therefore had, among other things, full access to educational opportunities. After the Second World War having citizenship became important, because Dutch citizens were entitled to migrate to the Netherlands. Many Indos 'went back' to the Netherlands although many had never been there before.[12] However, a substantial group stayed, by choice or because they were not allowed to go the Netherlands. This latter group is the focus of the present paper. The group of Indos now living in Indonesia (all Indonesian citizens) is culturally, socially and economically very diverse.[13] The informants we interviewed (see section 4) are a subset: economically and socially (lower) middle class and speaking Dutch to such an extent that they were able and prepared to be interviewed.

## 3    Dutch in Indonesia[14]

The status of the Dutch language in the Dutch East Indies was fundamentally different from English in the English colonies. The Dutch never tried to introduce Dutch as *the* language of the Dutch East Indies. Very little was invested

---

12    A relatively small group moved to Australia, Canada and the US.
13    De Vries (1976) gives an interesting description of the position of Dutch in the midseventies in Depok, a neighborhood of Djakarta where, before 1949, Dutch was spoken more frequently than elsewhere in Indonesia due to reasons described in Kwisthout (2007).
14    A substantial part of this section is based on Groeneboer (1994).

in Dutch education, at least up to the 20th century. In the second half of the 19th century, only a very limited group of non-Europeans received an education using Dutch as the language of transfer. Groeneboer (1994) mentioned that approximately only 0.012%, around 5,000 of the indigenous people, had an active command of Dutch. Instead, the use of Malay was encouraged. The Dutch focused on developing Malay as the lingua franca that could function as an effective means of governing the large and heterogeneous colony under one administrative system. Dutch was, of course, the language of governmental bodies, the judiciary, education, and the army.

This changed in the 20th century. More was invested in education, and the Dutch developed a language policy. Education in the Dutch East Indies in the first part of the 20th century was, obviously, class-oriented, as it was in the Netherlands, and race-oriented. Children of the social elite had access to the European primary school (*Europeesche Lagere School*). Teachers there often came from the Netherlands and the curriculum was the same. Indo-Europeans had access to these schools, but in practice the European schools were only accessible to those who already had a good command of Dutch. Non-European Indos and Chinese, belonging to the social middle class could go to the Dutch-indigenous schools (*Hollands-Inlandse Scholen*)[15] or the Dutch-Chinese schools (*Hollands-Chinese Scholen*). The language of instruction in these schools was a mix of Dutch and Malay or the local language. Many children only attended village schools offering three years of education. The opportunities for secondary schooling or higher education were very limited. Children could attend the MULO (*Meer Uitgebreid Lager Onderwijs*, literally 'more advanced primary education'),[16] although this was very expensive. The elite (Europeans, white or Indo's, or Chinese) could send their children to the HBS (*Hogere Burgerschool*, literally 'Higher Civic School'),[17] but only in a small number of cities. Those who could afford it sent their child to the Netherlands, which was rarely an option for Indos.

If possible, European Indos in the Dutch East Indies opted for a European education to give their children optimal opportunities. Proficiency in Dutch was a key to social success. Under these circumstances some parents chose to speak Dutch with their children, either because they also spoke Dutch at home when they were young, at work (as teachers or civil servants), or because they

---

15   Note that the word *Hollands* was back then used more often to refer to the Netherlands than nowadays. Many of the interviewees use both *Hollands* or *Nederlands* referring to the language.
16   Comparable with junior high school in the US education system.
17   Secondary education that gave access to university education.

wanted to give their children the opportunity to access European education. The choice of Dutch expressed social status and increased the social opportunities in the pre-Second World War colonial society.

In 1942 the Dutch East Indies were occupied by the Japanese. The Japanese abolished Dutch (and English) in public life in the Dutch East Indies in their fight against Western culture. Dutch-language education was banned with immediate effect. Indigenous schools were reopened on April 29, 1942, the birthday of Emperor Hirohito, preferably with Japanese and Malay as the language of instruction instead of Dutch or one of the national languages. This not only affected the Dutch, but also the Indo-Europeans, the Indonesian and Chinese elite, for whom Dutch was the mother tongue or second language. After all, for a very long time Dutch had been the only official language, politically and administratively, as well as socially. It was the language in which they had been trained and in which they often thought and expressed themselves. Many of the Indonesian nationalists used it despite the ideal of developing Malay into the unitary language *Bahasa Indonesia*.[18]

In 1945 Indonesian independence was declared. This, of course, changed the situation, even though the formal transfer of sovereignty only happened in 1949, after a four year armed conflict (*Agresi Militer Belanda*). Dutch lost its status as a means of increasing social opportunities. On the Dutch side, the acting Governor-General Van Mook made it known on November 6, 1945 that the Indonesian language would be further developed "so that the entire social, cultural and economic life can use it as its working language. The recognition of the Indonesian language as an official language alongside Dutch will be fully implemented" (Van der Wal 1971, 590; our translation). With this, the recognition on the Dutch side of Indonesian as an official language alongside Dutch was a fact. In 1947 the Dutch government gave Malay (later to become Bahasa Indonesia) the status of official language. Coulmas (1985, 245) notes that reintroduction of Dutch as an elite language did not materialize, partly because the Netherlands recognized the Indonesian language as the second official language in addition to Dutch.

All in all, after the Japanese occupation, Dutch was used less and less in social life. After the transfer of sovereignty, in 1949, it was replaced by Bahasa Indonesia as the language of instruction in education and management. Dutch

---

18   Foulcher (2000), Zentz (2017) noted that the (mainly Dutch-educated) nationalists who convened the All-Indonesia Youth Congress in Batavia (now Jakarta) in 1928 spoke mostly Dutch among themselves, and that their Malay communicative competence was limited.

organizations such as societies and associations disappeared. Before the war Malay was the language of those who stood up against colonial occupation (Anderson 1966, 139), after the war it was transformed into the official national language: Bahasa Indonesia ('language of Indonesia').[19] The Dutch language was abolished in 1950 in public primary education. A year later, the same thing happened in secondary education. Later on, in 1957 president Sukarno banned any form of education with Dutch as the language of instruction due to a conflict between Indonesia and the Netherlands about (Western) New Guinea, and the distribution of Dutch-language books and magazines through bookstores and publishers affiliated with the Netherlands stopped.

## 4 Speaking Dutch and Identity

In this section we report on a content analysis of a series of interviews and small focus groups conducted in the speech community described above. The interviews were originally meant to record the variety of Dutch spoken in Indonesia for linguistic purposes and were not specifically geared towards the topic of language and identity. Still, the content of the interviews and the context in which they took place, offered a wealth of information about the topics of identity, language and belonging, which will be analysed below.

### 4.1 Our Informants

Between July 2014 and May 2018, Dorien Theuns and Anne-France Pinget (both called 'I' for *interviewer* below) interviewed approximately 50 persons on the island of Java, in the cities Bandung, Jakarta/Depok, Malang/Batu, Semarang and Surabaya. As indicated above, our informants were elderly (generally 70+ years old at the time of the interview) and linguistically quite diverse. The interviewees were born between 1919 and 1947, with a majority between 1930 and 1947. (We identify them with M(ale)/F(emale)*year of birth). Some of the speakers can be called simultaneous bilinguals: they were born and raised in a bilingual environment, with mostly Dutch at home; and Malay, and/or indigenous languages like Javanese, Sundanese, or Madurese in public. Other speakers are early bilinguals: they learned Dutch at a young age when their primary school started. In short, all of them learned Dutch from a very early age, if not from birth.

---

19  Even though after 1949, Dutch was abolished as the language of education and administration, the political and cultural elite still spoke Dutch. Anderson (1966, 138) even writes: "To this day the vague line dividing those who are *binnen* (in) and those who are *buiten* (out) in Jakarta politics remains fluency in the colonial language."

The interviews took place in standard Dutch. While many speakers showed a (near-)native proficiency level, for instance because of relatives living in the Netherlands with whom they were in regular contact, some of them were not very fluent, but still perfectly able to answer our questions. In some interviews informants used Dutch-English code switching (see for example Excerpt 14). The use of code-switching may provide additional information about the speakers' opinions and identity. For some speakers, code switching seems to be an integral part of the variety they speak. We noted, however, that code switching in this data is often the consequence of word finding problems. Speakers with a lower level of Dutch proficiency often came up with an English word when they failed to retrieve the Dutch equivalent fast enough. It is beyond the scope of this article to investigate the code switching strategies in these data, which will be the subject of future work. The current analysis only focusses on content.

Interviews were orthographically transcribed. We left out hesitations, but we did leave the character of spoken language (with mistakes, unfinished sentences) intact. Parts of the conversations that were not directly relevant for a content analysis are marked with [...]. In this way the transcripts illustrate the variety of Dutch spoken by the interviewees. We here provide a content analysis centring on the topics of education (section 4.2), Dutch proficiency and inner speech (section 4.3), opposition between social groups (section 4.4), the importance of names (section 4.5), and *kumpulans* (section 4.6).[20]

### 4.2  Education and Upbringing

To understand the relationship between the Dutch language and identities in this speech community, it is crucial to examine what role Dutch played in the upbringing of the interviewees. In the colonial period the level of proficiency in Dutch in part defined one's position in society. Not every parent or caretaker could provide a Dutch environment from birth for their children, but all realized that proficiency in Dutch was a key to social success. Therefore, some opted, when able to opt, for a European education to optimize their children's opportunities. This is the case with M*1939.

Excerpt 1 shows that M*1939 grew up with his grandmother, who was a speaker of Sundanese. He gained access to Dutch through formal education starting when he was around five years old.

---

20   We do not indicate where the Dutch spoken is not fully 'correct' to keep the focus on the content. Only potentially confusing utterances are explained in footnotes. Translations are often quite literal.

# SPEAKING DUTCH IN INDONESIA: LANGUAGE AND IDENTITY

TABLE 11.1    Excerpt 1

| Transcription of the interview | English translation |
| --- | --- |
| M*1939: Wij zijn eigenlijk, ja wij noemen onszelf een Indo ja ... De omgeving bij ons thuis, mijn oma enzo ja, dat zijn allemaal Soendanezen, dus inheemsen van hier. Ik heb zelf mijn Hollandse taal pas op mijn vijfde jaar geleerd, want ik moest naar zo'n school. [...] Hollandse school, want thuis, ik was altijd bij mijn oma, spraken we Soendanees. [...] Maar met mijn vader thuis, die spreekt wel Nederlands [with a foster family; his parents left Indonesia, leaving him behind] | M*1939: We are actually, yes we call ourselves Indos yes ... The environment at our home, my grandmother and so on, they are all Sundanese, so indigenous people from here. I myself only learned the Dutch language at the age of five, because I had to go to this school. [...] a Dutch school, because at home, I was always with my grandmother, we spoke Sundanese. [...] But with my father at home, he does speak Dutch [with a foster family; his parents left Indonesia, leaving him behind] |

F*1944 in Excerpt 2 and F*1931 in Excerpt 3 explain that Dutch was the (only) way to achieve status in the pre-Second World War colonial society and increased social opportunities. F*1931 acknowledges that adopting Dutch as a native language also reproduced colonial patterns.

TABLE 11.2    Excerpt 2

| | |
| --- | --- |
| F*1944: Duitsers, Engelsen, Fransen, die spraken allemaal vloeiend Nederlands. Mijn vader heeft Nederlands geleerd, en hij was daar heel goed in, en hij heeft mij dus daarom altijd, wat is het, op een Nederlandse school gezet, vanaf kleinsaf en er ook echt op gelet dat ik Nederlands sprak. | F*1944: Germans, English, French: they all spoke fluent Dutch. My father learned Dutch, and he was very good at it, and that's why he always put me, what is it, into a Dutch school, from childhood onwards and really made sure that I spoke Dutch. |

TABLE 11.3  Excerpt 3

| | |
|---|---|
| F* 1931: Als je geen Nederlands sprak, dan ben je niets. Echt waar ... Dat is niet goed he, kolonialisme. We keken toch echt neer op hen ... Niet dat we op hen neerkeken, maar wij dachten dat hoort zo. Niet wetende, dat is politiek ja. | F* 1931: If you didn't speak Dutch, you are nothing. Really ... That's not good, eh, colonialism. We really looked down on them ... Not that we looked down on them, but we thought this is the way things are. Not knowing, that's politics, yes. |
| I: Dus uw ouders wilden dat u Nederlands sprak? | I: So your parents wanted you to speak Dutch? |
| F* 1931: Dat is onze moedertaal! | F* 1931: That's our mother tongue! |

For M* 1939 making the language his own, and marrying a person who also was able to speak Dutch (being *Indisch*; cf. footnote 11), meant being able to speak Dutch till this day:

TABLE 11.4  Excerpt 4

| | |
|---|---|
| M* 1939: Ja, misschien 70 jaar geleden heb ik die taal geleerd. | M* 1939: Yes, maybe 70 years ago I learned that language. |
| I: heeft u uw leven lang Nederlands gesproken of zijn er periodes geweest dat u het niet gesproken heeft? | I: Have you spoken Dutch all your life or have there been periods when you did not speak it? |
| M* 1939: Nee, toevallig is mijn vrouw een Indische ... dus wij spreken Nederlands. | M* 1939: No, my wife happens to be Indisch ... so we speak Dutch. |
| I: en nu vandaag de dag, hoe vaak spreekt u nog Nederlands? | I: and nowadays, how often do you still speak Dutch? |
| M* 1939: ja, met mijn vrouw. | M* 1939: yes, with my wife. |

However, after the Japanese invasion of the Dutch East Indies, Dutch was banned and abruptly replaced by Malay in daily life (see section 3). For some this had huge consequences. They did not only have to learn a new language but also had to change their identity, to become someone else. They migrated

# SPEAKING DUTCH IN INDONESIA: LANGUAGE AND IDENTITY 13

without moving. F*1919 in Excerpt 5, for instance, wanted to become teacher in a school for Indos, but she changed her mind when Dutch was banned as a language of instruction.

TABLE 11.5   Excerpt 5

| F*1919: In het begin was het onderwijs wel aantrekkelijk, maar later—toen we geen Hollands meer mochten spreken—toen moesten wij Indonesisch leren en daar had ik geen zin in. | F*1919: At first the [field of] education was attractive, but later—when we were no longer allowed to speak Dutch—we had to learn Indonesian and I didn't feel like it. |
|---|---|

TABLE 11.6   Excerpt 6

| F*1922: En toen kwamen de Japanners en dan was het uit … natuurlijk verschrikkelijk. Hoeveel … 4 jaar geen school—nothing. En ik heb Indonesisch moeten leren […] oh boy je kreeg klappen hoor van de lerares als je Hollands gebruikte. | F*1922: And then the Japanese came and then it was over … of course terrible. How many … no school for 4 years—nothing. And I had to learn Indonesian […] oh boy you got hit by the teacher if you used Dutch. |
|---|---|

M*1930 says in Excerpt 7 that in everyday life, outside the home, he spoke Javanese, and explains that his Dutch deteriorated because he did not use it much. In Excerpt 8 F*1942 explains that she has been living 'in two worlds': her early education was in Dutch, but she attended an Indonesian secondary school. After 1958 they had to speak Indonesian. Both indicate that they spoke Dutch less and less. They did not pass it on to their children as M*1930 explains:

TABLE 11.7   Excerpt 7

| M*1930: Wij zijn opgevoed in het Nederlands. […] Vader sprak Nederlands met ons, moeder sprak gebroken Nederlands met ons. Maar wel opgevoed op zijn Nederlands.[…] Maar door de jaren … beetje een beetje vergeten omdat we vaak Indonesisch praten, en soms met de kinderen ook Javaans praten. | M*1930: We were raised in Dutch. […] Father spoke Dutch with us, mother spoke broken Dutch with us. But raised the Dutch way. […] But over the years … a bit forgotten, because we often speak Indonesian, and sometimes also speak Javanese with the children. |
|---|---|

TABLE 11.8  Excerpt 8

| | |
|---|---|
| I: Kunt u wat vertellen over het onderwijs dat u heeft gehad toen u jong was? | I: Can you tell us a bit about your education when you were young? |
| F* 1942: Ja dus, ik heb de lagere school gehad … de lagere school Nederlands. En daarom eh, leef ik eigenlijk nou in tweeën. | F* 1942: Yes so, I went to primary school … primary Dutch school. And that's why I actually live in two worlds. |
| I: Kunt u vertellen hoe u uw eigen identiteit destijds zag. Zag u zichzelf als Nederlander of als Indo, of Indisch, of als Indonesisch? Hoe moet ik me dat voorstellen? | I: Can you tell us how you perceived your own identity at the time? Did you see yourself as Dutch or as Indo, or Indisch, or as Indonesian? How should I picture that? |
| F* 1942: Ik probeerde me altijd als Indonesische voor te stellen. Ik probeerde me bij de Indonesiërs te gedragen als een Indonesiër. Maar, je voelde toch dat er een verschil is. Dat ze je toch anders aankijken. Niet direct één van hun. Ja, ik ben van huis uit natuurlijk heel erg Nederlands opgevoed. Ik heb ook de Nederlandse school gehad. Maar daarna was ik getrouwd. Mijn man sprak ook wel Nederlands, maar de anderen spraken natuurlijk allemaal Indonesisch. | F* 1942: I always tried to introduce myself as Indonesian. I tried to behave like an Indonesian with Indonesians. However, you still felt that there is a difference. That they look at you differently. Not directly one of them. Yes, of course I was raised very Dutch. I also went to a Dutch school. But after that I was married. My husband also spoke Dutch, but of course the others all spoke Indonesian. |

### 4.3   Dutch Proficiency and Inner Speech

The examples below illustrate that for some of our interviewees Dutch was and is their native language, the language in which they express themselves best. F* 1937 says "I always think in Dutch." Like F* 1922, she explains that Dutch is the language for inner speech, i.e. the language used for thinking, analyzing, counting, etc.

TABLE 11.9  Excerpt 9

| | |
|---|---|
| F* 1922: Maar er is een ding dat mij bij gebleven is. En dat is dat ik toch—nog altijd—de dingen kan analyseren in het | F* 1922: But there is one thing that sticks in my mind. And that is that I can—still— analyze things in Dutch. […] All these |

# SPEAKING DUTCH IN INDONESIA: LANGUAGE AND IDENTITY

TABLE 11.9  Excerpt 9 *(cont.)*

| | |
|---|---|
| Hollands. [...] Al die jaren ben ik niet in staat om met een Hollander te spreken. Gek is dat ... Het is eigenaardig maar de taal blijf je bij hoor. | years I have not been able to speak to a Dutchman. It is strange ... It is peculiar, but the language remains with you. |

TABLE 11.10  Excerpt 10

| | |
|---|---|
| F* 1931: Maar ik kan vrijer uitdrukken ja in het Engels of in het Hollands ... en in het Indonesisch wordt het een beetje stijf volgens mij. | F* 1931: But I can express more freely yes in English or in Dutch ... and in Indonesian it gets a bit stiff I think. |

TABLE 11.11  Excerpt 11

| | |
|---|---|
| F* 1938–2: En dat optellen, opsommen van wat betaald moet worden, is voor mij moeilijk in het Indonesisch. Dan ben ik niet vlug genoeg. Doe ik het nog altijd in het Nederlands. Wil ik iets uitleggen, is voor mij soms in het Indonesisch een beetje moeilijk. Ja, dan doe ik het in Nederlands. | F* 1938–2: And this adding up, summing up what has to be paid, is difficult for me in Indonesian. Then I am not fast enough. I still do it in Dutch. If I want to explain something, it is sometimes a bit difficult for me in Indonesian. Yes, then I will do it in Dutch. |

For F* 1931 it is very difficult to admit that Dutch is her dominant language and that she does not feel that comfortable speaking Indonesian:

TABLE 11.12  Excerpt 12

| | |
|---|---|
| F* 1931: Ik kan me beter uitdrukken in het Hollands of zelfs in het Engels dan in het Indonesisch. [...] Nu nog steeds ... Eigenlijk is het niet zo leuk ... Dat hoort toch niet ... een andere taal leuker vinden dan je eigen [lands]taal. | F* 1931: I can express myself better in Dutch or even in English than in Indonesian. [...] Still now ... Actually, it is not that nice ... That shouldn't be ... liking another language more than your own [national] language. |

Almost all interviewees were Christians. In a religious context Dutch is sometimes used. Some pray in Dutch; F*1946 is not able to recite Hail Mary in Indonesian, even though she uses both Dutch and Indonesian in the family circle:

TABLE 11.13   Excerpt 13

| | |
|---|---|
| I: En hoe vaak spreekt u nog Nederlands? | I: And how often do you speak Dutch? |
| F*1946: Vaak [...] met mijn kleinkinderen, met mijn broer, mijn schoonzus, met de kinderen van mijn broer. | F*1946: Often [...] with my grandchildren, with my brother, my sister-in-law, with my brother's children. |
| I: Dus met vrienden en familie, allebei. Soms in de kerk ook nog? | I: So, with friends and family, both. Sometimes also in church? |
| F*1946: Ja, soms. | F*Yes, sometimes. |
| I: Gebruikt u de Nederlandse taal ook nog voor het bidden? | I: Do you also use the Dutch language for praying? |
| F*1946: Oh ja, wat is dat, twaalf artikelen van het geloof, ik kan niet in behasa,[21] zo, en Onze Vader ook. Dus ik moet eerst wennen Wees Gegroet Maria, ook alles in het Nederlands. | F*1946: Oh yes, what is that, twelve articles of faith, I can't [recite them] in behasa, so, and Our Father too. So I first have to get used Hail Mary, everything in Dutch too. |

### 4.4   *Sameness and Difference:* Us *and* Them

When Indonesia became independent, Dutch-speaking Indos had to adapt. For social acceptance they focused on Indonesian identity and customs, but they still remember their Dutch upbringing. Differences between European and Indonesian norms, values and customs are sometimes mentioned. Excerpts 18–20 illustrate that the interviewees sometimes live in two worlds, in two cultures, with a split identity:

---

21   Behasa Indonesia = Indonesian.

TABLE 11.14  Excerpt 14

| | |
|---|---|
| F* 1922: Je bent niet eens een Hollandse, je bent opgevoed met de Javanen, maar—het is een funny thing—sometimes I begin to doubt—waar hoor ik nog bij eigenlijk ... Ik zie geen Hollander hier, en ik ben helemaal geen Hollandse, maar waarom ... waarom denk ik zo in het Hollandse en analyseer ik het en ... hoe gek is dat? Waar hoor ik nou eigenlijk bij? | F* 1922: You're not even Dutch, you were raised with the Javanese, but—it's a funny thing—sometimes I begin to doubt—where do I actually belong ... I don't see any Dutch here, and I am not Dutch at all, but why ... why do I think so in the Dutch language and analyze it and ... how strange is that? Where do I actually belong? |

TABLE 11.15  Excerpt 15

| | |
|---|---|
| M* 1938: Want Nederlands-Indië, die hier wonen zijn toch Europeanen [...] Maar terwijl wij toen in Nederlands-Indië, wij zijn allemaal Nederlandse onderdaan. Wij spreken allemaal Nederlands. Maar ja, Nederland is, ja wat is dat, is niet, is onrechtvaardig. ... Wij zijn, wij leven in Indonesië maar zijn niet 100 % Indonesisch ... Wij zijn ex-Nederlanders. | M* 1938: Because the Dutch East Indies, who live here are Europeans after all [...] But while we were in the Dutch East Indies, we were all Dutch subjects. We all speak Dutch. But yes, the Netherlands is, yes what is that, is not, is unfair. ... We are, we live in Indonesia but are not 100 % Indonesian ... We are ex-Dutch. |

TABLE 11.16  Excerpt 16

| | |
|---|---|
| M* 1930: In het begin voelde ik mezelf meer Nederlands, maar nadat ik de Indonesische staatsburgerschap heb overgenomen, voel ik toch ook dat ik meer Indonesisch, aan de Indonesische kant sta ... Vaak zeg ik tegen mensen, uiterlijk ben ik Nederlander, maar innerlijk ben ik Indonesiër. | M* 1930: In the beginning I felt more Dutch, but after I took over Indonesian citizenship, I also feel that I am more Indonesian, stand on the Indonesian side ... I often say to people, I am Dutch on the outside, but on the inside I am Indonesian. |

F*1938–1 explains that Sukarno went to a Dutch school and could speak Dutch very well, just like many of his ministers. She uses it as an example to show that those who are proficient in Dutch find it impossible to avoid using the language:

TABLE 11.17  Excerpt 17

| F*1938–1: Maar als je nou eenmaal gewend bent om Nederlands te spreken, geloof je dat je dus .... Want mijn vriendinnen, ja, die altijd Nederlands hebben gesproken. Als je ontmoet dan spreek je gewoon Nederlands. Je hebt wel, ja, paar collega's van mij die geen Nederlands kunnen spreken, die worden dus een beetje krengerig,[22] begrijp je. "Ach jij met je Hollands spreken, zeg."[23] | F*1938–1: But once you are used to speaking Dutch, you believe that you .... Because my friends, yes, who have always spoken Dutch. When you meet you just speak Dutch. There is, yes, few colleagues of mine who cannot speak Dutch, so they get a bit bothered, you understand. "Oh you, speaking Dutch again." |
|---|---|

Later on, F*1938–1 says that a friend who was a lawyer was not allowed to speak Dutch by his father. This friend told her: "mijn vader is een echte Indonesiër. Hij wil niet dat wij Nederlands spreken." (My father is a real Indonesian. He doesn't want us to speak Dutch).

M*1939 recounts that he was drafted into the army to fight against the Dutch.[24] His description of what happened points to a feeling of 'us' and 'them':

TABLE 11.18  Excerpt 18

| I: En toen zat u bij het Indonesische leger? | I: And then you were in the Indonesian army? |
|---|---|
| M*1939: Ja. Marine. [...] | M*1939: Yes. Navy. [...] |

---

22   Literally, 'bitchy' In present-day Dutch we would not use that word in this context, but use the word *geïrriteerd* (irritated).
23   Note that she uses the present tense, but she talks about the past. This seems to be a typical feature of the Dutch spoken by this group and can be observed in many excerpts.
24   In 1949 Indonesia became independent but one part of the Dutch East Indies stayed Dutch territory: *Nederlands Nieuw Guinea* (Netherlands New Guinea). The Indonesian govern-

TABLE 11.18 Excerpt 18 (*cont.*)

| | |
|---|---|
| I: Maar in Nieuw-Guinea toen moest u dus, eh, dat was tijdens kwestie van Nieuw-Guinea | I: But in New Guinea you had to, eh that was during the New Guinea crisis |
| M* 1939: van Nieuw-Guinea ja | M* 1939: New Guinea yes |
| I: met Nederland, dus toen moest u eigenlijk tegen de Hollanders | I: and the Netherlands, so then you actually had to go against the Dutch |
| M* 1939: Ja ik moest tegen de Hollanders gaan vechten [laughs] | M* 1939: Yes I had to fight the Dutch [laughs] |
| I: Maar u was in feite opgegroeid als Indische jongen? | I: But you actually grew up as an Indische boy? |
| M* 1939: Ja | M* 1939: Yes |
| I: Maar voor uw gevoel van identiteit, u accepteerde maar dat u nu opeens aan de Indonesische kant stond tegenover de Hollanders, of heeft u zich nooit zo erg aan de Hollandse kant gevoeld? | I: But for your sense of identity, you accepted that you were suddenly on the Indonesian side against the Dutch, or have you never felt so much on the Dutch side? |
| M* 1939: Nou ook niet zo erg ja. Want ja wij wij zijn eigenlijk, wij noemen onszelf dan Indo's hier hè. Dus hè de omgeving bij ons thuis vanaf mijn oma enzo ja, [die] zijn allemaal Soendanese, dus inheemse van hier. [...] Dus natio- over nationaliteit ook niet zo erg ja. Ja wel de vrienden denk je maar toen ach. Nee, ook niet zo erg hoor. Want het is nooit tot een contact gekomen. | M* 1939: Well not really either. Because yes, we we are actually, we call ourselves Indos here right. So, right the environment at our home from my grandmother onwards you know yes, [they] are all Sundanese, so native from here. [...] So not so much about natio- nationality either, yes. Yes, the friends you think but then well. No, not really. Because it never came to a contact [a fight]. |

ment did not accept that. This culminated in hostilities in 1962. The conflict almost leads to war, but under great pressure from the United Nations, New Guinea is handed over to Indonesia on 1 May 1963.

The following excerpt illustrates that not only do the interviewees use Dutch instead of Indonesian, the way in which they interact differs as well. F*1938–2 talks about a conversation she had, in Indonesian, but the way she interacts is 'Dutch-like':

TABLE 11.19  Excerpt 19

| F*1938–2: [Er] wordt misschien iets besproken, en je bent met dat gesprek niet overeen, en dan kom je zeggen, nou dan het toch zo moeten zijn […] Waarom doe je dit niet. Dat is te vlug, mag ik niet doen. | F*1938–2: Maybe something is being discussed, and you don't agree with that conversation, and then you say, well it should have been like this […] Why don't you do this. That's too fast, I am not allowed to do it. |
|---|---|
| I: Te Nederlands | I: Too Dutch |
| F*1938–2: Ja, dat mag niet. Ik ben te accuraat,[25] dat mag niet. Kan je het niet kalmer zeggen, zeggen ze dan. Kan je het niet in andere woorden uitleggen. Zie je, en dan wordt het voor ons moeilijk. | F*1938–2: Yes, that is not allowed. I'm too direct, that's not allowed. Can't you say it calmer, they say. Can't you explain it in other words. You see, and then it gets difficult for us. |

### 4.5  Names

When Suharto came to power in 1967, he wanted everyone in Indonesia to adopt the same national identity. His 'New Order' was also strongly anti-Communist. Minorities with a migration background had to adapt and Chinese Indonesians in particular were suffering. Changing Chinese names to Indonesian names was first recommended and later legally required. This law was part of a series of measures and laws to eclipse Chinese identity.

The pressure on minorities was also felt by Indos. Changing their names was not required by law, but it made getting a job as civil servants much easier, for example. It also put less emphasis on their European background, which facilitated social acceptance by their Indonesian environment. There were Indos who therefore changed their names, but also Indos who were proud of their European background and kept their names.

---

25   She uses *accuraat* (accurate), but we think she means *direct, precies* (direct, precise). It is one of these things that distinguishes Indos from Indonesians (in the eyes of some of our interviewees): being accurate, disciplined, on time.

TABLE 11.20 Excerpt 20

M*1946 (clearly Dutch first and last name): Maar iedereen vraag aan mij van waar is dat pak[26] [last name] [...] dus voor mij is dat gemakkelijk. Ik kwam erin met die naam, maar geen probleem voor mij.

I: Zijn er andere mensen die er wel een probleem mee hebben gehad?

M*1946: Ja, veel. Als je een Hollandse naam had, verwissel de naam. Je hebt een zeker [Dutch last name] een vriend van mij, hij verandert zijn naam naar Abdul X.

I. Wanneer?

M*1946: In jaar 60 zo ongeveer, hij verandert de naam. Dus, een paar gebruiken de naam niet meer. En een paar zijn ook verlegen om de naam te gebruiken. Je moet aan Willem Y vragen; hij gaat altijd rond, en hij vindt altijd die arme Indo's die hier zijn in Soerabaja, ze verwisselen de naam, ze zijn verlegen om die naam te gebruiken. En ook niet geschikt, want ze wonen in de kampong.

I. Wat bedoelt u met 'niet geschikt'?

M*1946: Omdat ze in de kampong wonen en om met die naam rond te lopen is ook moeilijk [...] dus om bijeen te komen met de mensen van de kampong, zodat ze geen verschil maken, ja, velen verwisselen de naam.

M*1946: But everyone asks me why is that mister [last name] ... so for me that is easy. I came in with that name, but no problem for me.

I: Are there other people who thought it problematic?

M*1946: Yes a lot. If you had a Dutch name, switch the name. You have a so-called [Dutch last name], a friend of mine, he changes his name to Abdul X.

I. When?

M*1946: In the year 1960 approximately, he changes the name. So, a few don't use the name anymore. And a few are shy about using the name too. You have to ask Willem Y; he always goes around, and he always thinks those poor Indos who are here in Surabaya, they change the name, they are shy to use that name. And not suitable either, because they live in the kampong [village].

I. What do you mean by 'not suitable'?

M*1946: Because they live in the kampong and to walk around with that name is also difficult [...] so to get together with the people of the kampong, so they are not different [from others] yes, many change the name.

26   *pak* is Indonesian for 'mister.'

TABLE 11.21 Excerpt 21

| | |
|---|---|
| M*1930: Van daaruit heb ik een job gekregen, als ambtenaar bij de belastingkantoor. Maar ik moet mijn naam veranderen. Dat heb ik gedaan. Dat was in 1980. Als ik mijn naam niet verander dan kan ik niet binnenkomen. Als ze praat over Nederlands, vind ik ook niet leuk. | M*1930: From there I got a job, as a civil servant at the tax office. But I have to change my name. I have done that. That was in 1980. If I don't change my name then I can't come in. When they talk about Dutch, I don't like it. |
| I: als uw collega's ... | I: when your colleagues ... |
| M*1930: Ja collega's, mijn collega's, oh je diploma's allemaal *londo*.[27] Daar word ik kwaad van. Als zij zeggen *londo*. Moet ik weer rustig [...] Niet alleen Nederlands, ja die moeten veranderen, ja, naam, ook Chinezen, naam veranderen. Maar zodra ze overleden zijn, hun echte naam kom tevoorschijn. | M*1930: Yes colleagues, my colleagues, oh your diplomas all *londo*.[19] This makes me angry. When they say *londo*. I have to calm down again [...] Not only [those with a] Dutch [name], yes they have to change, yes, name, but also Chinese, [they have to] change name. But once they die, their real name comes out. |
| I: op het graf, bedoelt u? | I: on the grave, you mean? |
| M*1930: Ja, dat is zo, op het graf. | M*1930: Yes, true, on the grave. |

### 4.6 Kumpulans

Hewitt (2016) describes how, after the fall of Suharto in 1998, identity politics in Indonesia changed. It was safe (again) to speak Dutch and many Indos started to do this again. On their retirement, many reconnect with their youth, and Indo clubs and *kumpulans* have sprung up in many cities on Java. A kumpulan is a social gathering with peers, enjoying food, talk about the past, and speaking Dutch. Anyone who speaks Dutch, Indo or not, is welcome.

---

27  The word *londo*, term of abuse, is derived from *Belondo* in Javanese, it means *Belanda* in Indonesian meaning 'Dutch' or 'the Dutch people.'

# SPEAKING DUTCH IN INDONESIA: LANGUAGE AND IDENTITY

The daily life and the identity of Indos in Indonesia have become quite different from those of their relatives who left. Children and grandchildren who grew up in Indonesia rather than in the Dutch East Indies, hardly ever speak Dutch. The Indos we spoke usually felt primarily Indonesian. At these kumpulans it often happens that Indonesian songs are sung in addition to Dutch songs. Dishes are also served that have both a Western and Indonesian flavor.

Following Kuiper (2005) these kumpulans could be described as 'language sanctuaries.' The idea of a sanctuary is of a sociocultural locus of safety, comparable to medieval usage, when a person pursued by the civil authorities could seek sanctuary in a church where canon law applied. The sanctuary was both a physical location, such as a church, and a sociocultural locus where the church laid down the rules. So, a language sanctuary, as Kuiper conceptualizes it, is a socio-cultural locus where a language could safely be used free from those influences which would lead to its endangerment.

M*1930 in Excerpt 22 describes a Dutch 'conversation club' in Malang, called NCCM:

TABLE 11.22 Excerpt 22

| | |
|---|---|
| M*1930: Wij gaan naar de NCCM, de Nederlandse Conversatie Club Malang, ... elke maand hebben wij een bijeenkomst. [...] Het is gewoon een culturele groep hoor, het is niet dat wij georiënteerd zijn op Nederland. Nee, helemaal niet. Het moet alleen omdat wij die taal hebben geleerd, en wij willen die taal behouden. Want als je een taal niet aldoor spreekt dan vergeet je veel. Je vergeet woorden, zoals ik nu spreek, is het soms een beetje moeilijk om naar woorden te zoeken. | M*1930: We go to the NCCM, the Dutch Conversation Club Malang ... every month we have a meeting. [...] It is just a cultural group, it is not the case that we are oriented towards the Netherlands. No not at all. It is only necessary because we have learned that language, and we want to maintain that language. Because if you don't speak a language all the time, you forget a lot. You forget words, as I speak now, it is sometimes a bit difficult to find the words. |

M*1930 showed (on video) during the interview the songs they sing during these meetings, a mix of Dutch and Indonesian songs. They start with the national anthem, *Indonesia Raya*. He then sings the club song "Wij zijn weer tezamen, de NCCM, ..." (We are together again, the NCCM). Other songs mentioned are "De rozen die bloeien" (The roses that blossom) and "Indonesia mijn geboorteland" (Indonesia, my country of birth).

The following excerpt comes from an interview with a few women, just before their kumpulan starts (we have their names, but not their year of birth).

TABLE 11.23 Excerpt 23

---

F1: Ons groepje, onze vereniging, heet Rendez-Vous, een wederontmoeting die we iedere maand, komen we dan bij elkaar. En dan brengen we wat lekkers, ieder brengt wat mee

F1: Our group, our association, is called Rendez-Vous, reconvening every month, we then get together. And then we bring something tasty, everyone brings something

F2: Hoeveel jaren bestaat het al?

F2: For how many years?

F1: 28 januari 2005, waren wij begonnen.

F1: 28 January 2005, we started.

I: Kunt u misschien vertellen waarom u negen jaar geleden dit groepje heeft opgericht?

I: Could you maybe explain why you started this group nine years ago?

F1: Ja, kijk daar zijn al zo veel Indischen weg van Indonesië, en als je telt hoeveel Indischen, zo weinig toch? Dus hadden we het idee om ja echt goede vrienden bij elkaar te roepen, bijeen te komen, om elkaar te helpen, als we raad nodig hebben, of ja

F1: Yes, you see so many Indischen have already left Indonesia, and if you count how many Indischen, so few, right? So, we had the idea, yes, to call together really good friends, to get together, to help each other, if we need advice, or yes

F3: dus om contact te houden met elkaar, ja, iedere maand komen we bij elkaar

F3: so, to keep in touch, yes, every month we get together

F1: en dat ons Hollands, onze Hollandse taal niet weggaat he, want dat is voornaam, want dat is onze moedertaal, toch

F1: and that our Dutch, our Dutch language won't go away, right, because that is important, because that is our mother tongue, isn't it

---

## 5 Concluding Remarks: The End of the Colonial Era[28]

This paper explored the linguistic and cultural situation of a substantial group of Indonesian state citizens who acquired Dutch at a very early age. After the independence, these citizens (mostly, but not exclusively, of Eurasian descent) stayed in Indonesia, either by choice or because they were not allowed to migrate to the Netherlands. Using a content analysis of a dozen interviews drawn from a dataset of around 50 interviews, we outlined the role the Dutch language plays in our interviewees' sense of identity.

We showed that the identity of this group is intrinsically related to the status of the Dutch language in the society. They initially made every effort to learn Dutch as children and/or at school, and in doing so aimed to be integrated into the highest strata of the Dutch colonial society. Being able to speak Dutch, and, therefore, being able to internalize a European(-like) education was closely connected to the fact that they either were Dutch citizens or became Dutch citizens.

Things changed drastically immediately after the Second World War. The Dutch-speaking Indos we interviewed were often not considered real Indonesians. They were confronted with limited acceptance by society and were given fewer opportunities because of their social characteristics. This affected their sense of identity. Due to their Dutch way of life in the Dutch East Indies, they had a higher social status than the indigenous Indonesians. In the new Indonesia, roles became reversed: they were often disadvantaged and stigmatized exactly because of their social and linguistic connection with the Dutch colonial authority. Immediately after independence president Sukarno prioritized Indonesians on the labor market. Afterwards there was a period in which it was forbidden to speak Dutch. This was often an incentive for interviewees to choose the Indonesian nationality, to change their names and their career perspectives, and often to give up speaking Dutch outside their homes and not pass it on to their children.

After the fall of Suharto in 1998, identity politics changed. Speaking Dutch (in public places) was accepted again. Many Indos started to do this (cf. section 4.6) and learned about their origins by looking back on their youth. When Indos use Dutch nowadays, they actively reveal their identity and their past experiences. With every speech act individual speakers perform an "act of iden-

---

28    We cannot stress enough that our concluding remarks are based on our (limited) dataset. What we found, fits in with what is said in Bosma et al. (2006) and Hewitt (2016), but the reader should be cautious in generalizing what we observed to hold for all those of Eurasian descent.

tity" (Le Page 1986), revealing through their use of language their sense of social and ethnic solidarity or difference. At present, this speech community, which is slowly dying out, have split or ambiguous identities, their feelings ranging from pride to a lack of belonging. Yet the majority of Indos we interviewed clearly identified themselves as Indonesians and would not want to live elsewhere.

This study illustrates the multilingual approach to intercultural language contact, analyzing how individuals deal with multilingual and multicultural situations. Furthermore, it underlines the relevance of linguistic anthropological research, in which group membership is investigated in linguistic terms, next to the equally relevant social, cultural, historical and political terms (Silverstein 1996). Looking at language status, use, practises and ideologies, we showed that the Dutch language reflects the split or ambiguous identity of a speech community. We shed light on clashes reflected by language between 1) this speech community and other groups in the Indonesian society, 2) clashes at the individual level between past and present language practices, and 3) current clashes when individuals manoeuvre within different situations. To conclude, the investigation of Dutch as spoken in Indonesia, which was conducted in the current paper in an explorative manner, turned out to be highly relevant in order to understand how language can be constitutive of social identities constructed both at the community and individual level.

### References

Anderson, Benedict. "The Languages of Indonesian Politics." *Indonesia* 1 (1966): 89–116.
Anderson, Benedict. "Review: Becoming Dutch, Staying Indo." *Inside Indonesia* 103 (2011). Accessed February 19, 2021. http://www.insideIndonesia.org/review-becoming-dutchstaying-Indo.
Annink, Carol. "*Orang Indo* en *Indonesian-Dutch*: Indische Nederlanders in Indonesië en de Verenigde Staten van Amerika." In *Het Onbekende Vaderland: de Repatriëring van Indische Nederlanders (1946–1964)*, edited by Wim Willems and Leo Lucassen, 147–171. 's-Gravenhage: Sdu Uitgeverij, 1994.
Beets, Gijs, Corina Huisman, Evert van Imhoff, Santo Koesoebjono, and Evelien Walhout. *De Demografische Geschiedenis van Indische Nederlanders*. Den Haag: Nederlands Interdisciplinair Demografisch Instituut, 2002.
Bosma, Ulbe, Remco Raben, and Wim Willems. *De Geschiedenis van Indische Nederlanders*. Amsterdam: B. Bakker 2006.
Bosma, Ulbe, and Remco Raben. *Being "Dutch" in the Indies. A History of Creolisation and Empire, 1500–1920*. Singapore/Ohio; Singapore University Press, Ohio University Press, 2008.

Bucholtz, Mary, and Kira Hall. Language and identity. *A Companion to Linguistic Anthropology* 1 (2004): 369–394.
Coulmas, Florian. *Sprache und Staat: Stidien zur Sprachplanung und Sprachpolitik.* Berlin/New York: De Gruyter, 1985.
De la Croix, Humphrey. (2013) "Eurasians of the Netherlands Indies: People in Diaspora (2)." *Latitudes* (2013). Accessed February 19, 2021. http://latitudes.nu/eurasians-of-the-netherlands-indies-people-in-diaspora-2/.
Foulcher, Keith. "SumpahPemuda: The Making and Meaning of a Symbol of Indonesian Nationhood." *Asian Studies Review* 24, no. 3 (2000): 377–410.
Groeneboer, Kees. *Weg tot het Westen: Het Nederlands voor Indië 1600–1950: Een Taalpolitieke Geschiedenis.* Leiden: KITLV, 1994.
Hewitt, Rosalind. "Indo (Eurasian) Communities in Postcolonial Indonesia." PhD diss., The Australian National University, 2016.
Kuiper, Koenraad. "Invisible Immigrants, Inaudible Language: Nederlands en Nederlanders in Nieuw Zeeland." In *Languages of New Zealand*, edited by Allan Bell, Ray Harlow and Donna Starks, 322–342. Wellington: Victoria University Press, 2005.
Kwisthout, Jan-Karel. *Sporen uit het verleden van Depok.* Woerden: Free Musketeers, 2007.
Le Page, Robert. "Acts of Identity." *English Today* 2, no. 4 (1986): 21–24.
Meijer, Hans. *In Indië Geworteld: de Twintigste Eeuw.* Amsterdam: B. Bakker, 2004.
Silverstein, Michael. "Encountering Languages and Languages of Encounter in North American Ethnohistory." *Journal of Linguistic Anthropology* 6, no. 2 (1996): 126–144.
Veer, Paul W. van der (1990). "Ongepubliceerd materiaal over Indische Nederlanders in het voormalig Nederlands-Indië." In *Indische Nederlanders in de ogen van de wetenschap*, edited by Wim Willems, 111–125. Leiden: Centrum voor Onderzoek van Maatschappelijke Tegenstellingen, 1990.
Vries, Jan de. "De Depokkers: geschiedenis, sociale structuur en taalgebruik van een geïsoleerde gemeenschap." *Bijdragen tot de Taal-, Land- en Volkenkunde* 132, no. 2/3 (1976): 228–248.
Wal, Simon Lambertus van der. *Officiële bescheiden betreffende de Nederlands-Indonesische betrekkingen 1945–1950.* 's-Gravenhage: Nijhoff, 1971–1986.
Zentz, Laren. *Statehood, Scale and Hierarchy. History, Language and Identity in Indonesia.* Bristol: Multilingual Matters, 2017.

CHAPTER 12

# The Effect of Migration on Identity: Sociolinguistic Research in a Plurilingual Setting

*Elisa Candido*

## 1          Introduction

Intercultural Communication can informally be defined as the use of language in a setting in which interlocutors are concerned with making the interaction positive and productive, although they do not share the same linguistic or cultural background. They are aware of their possible (non) verbal and cultural differences and use this awareness to improve mutual understanding. In a more general sense, Intercultural Communication can also be associated with sociolinguistics and language diversity, i.e. the use of different languages and/or dialects coexisting in the same society. These linguistic varieties sometimes belong to the same linguistic family and, for this reason, then tend to share certain grammatical features. The Albanian language, for instance, can be divided in two main dialects, Gheg and Tosk, spoken roughly north or south of the Shkumbin River, respectively as shown in Figure 12.1 (cf. Manzelli 2004).

Though identified as two different dialects, they share most lexical and morphosyntactic features. The divergence between the two linguistic varieties becomes visible at the phonological level. A child born in the north of the country is likely to call its mother *nan* and its father *babe*, whereas a child living in the south of the country will call its parents *nëne* and *babi*. Since standard Albanian is based on the Tosk dialect, both children will learn the latter pair of words in school and experience few problems when conversing (cf. Triolo 2006).

There are also societies in which languages and/or dialects belonging to different linguistic families coexist; these may be connected to different (in)formal domains /or they may be suitable for specific communicative events. A situation of this kind can be found in Italy, where phenomena like bi- and plurilingualism, diglossia and even dilalia are of the order of the day (cf. Dell'Aquila and Iannàccaro 2004 and 2006). Twelve of these linguistic varieties are recognized and protected by the Italian state. Three of these languages—together with Venetian—are spoken in north-eastern region Friuli Venezia-Giulia; and for this reason, part of the (individual) linguistic repertoire.

THE EFFECT OF MIGRATION ON IDENTITY

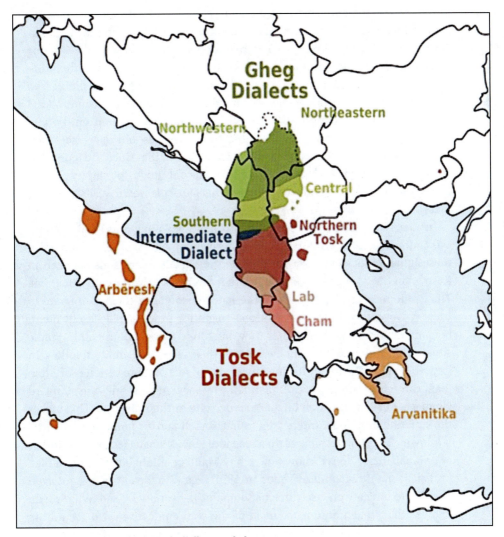

FIGURE 12.1    Geographic spread of Albanian dialects

The city of Maniago is situated in an area dominated by one of these minority languages, namely Friulian. This language is spoken almost throughout the region and, in contrast to Slovenian and German, has a large number of speakers, namely about 600,000 (cf. Orioles 2003). The figure does not show that 11,000 inhabitants have a linguistic repertoire that consists of three linguistic varieties. Though Friulian is seen as the town's original language, over time Venetian and Italian have enriched the local repertoire. Venetian was introduced as the language of the church, and the Venetian nobility moved to the territory in the sixteenth and later centuries because of economic opportunities the area offered. It became a language used in certain formal domains, while Friulian remained dominant in the informal and certain formal domains. For this reason, they were able to coexist for a long time without threatening each other (cf. Francescato 1991b). This is not true for Italian. Since the unification of the peninsula in 1861 the importance of the language has increased more and more. Its social prestige extended especially after the Second World War, with the introduction of the television. From this moment on the language increasingly threatened the other two languages and decreased their influence in the communicative sphere. It is believed that since the 1990s Italian, unlike the other two languages, has been the only linguistic variety present in every individual linguistic repertoire in this particular town (cf. Francescato 1991a).

In 2012, when the present research took place, 1280 migrants lived in Maniago, among them, 490 mother tongue speakers of Albanian. The majority of these inhabitants were born in Albania, though Albanian is also spoken in Kosovo and Macedonia. Their L1, in other words, is (a variety of) Albanian. The economic crisis in Albania in the 1990s encouraged them to migrate to Italy (cf. Devole 2006). In this traditional migration process, male family members migrated first, and only after they had found work, a house and a stable situation in which to build a new life, did their wives and children follow. In Italy, these people, already having knowledge of one or more varieties of Albanian, came into contact with Italian citizens speaking not only the standard language, but having a rich linguistic repertoire at their disposal. This makes the situation even more interesting from a sociolinguistic point of view. Little is known about the division of the three indigenous languages over the different domains, nor do we know how many Maniagese inhabitants are, in fact, proficient in Friulian and/or Venetian. With regard to the latter, it is not even possible to indicate precisely in what domains the variety is used. What we do know is that Italian dominates most of the communicative settings and the number of L1 speakers of this language, or rather regional Italian, increases with every generation. Young Friulians often also state they feel more attached to Italian than Friulian. This language enables them to express their feelings and thoughts best (cf. Picco 2001). This is also true for 65% of the Italian L1 speaking Maniaghese who participated as the control group in the research. These 23 women and 18 men in the 18–87 age range were asked to auto valuate their language skills for Friulian, Venetian and Italian.

As shown in Figure 12.2 all participants, members of the Albanian speech community, indicate they have developed good reading skills in Italian. Furthermore, and in line with the above discussion, they declare to have a high proficiency in the other three skills in the same language. Fewer Maniaghese

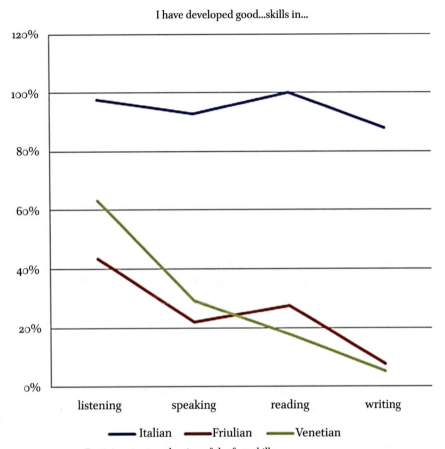

FIGURE 12.2    Participant auto valuation of the four skills

state they have developed a good range of linguistic skills for the two other languages, but the graph offers a very interesting insight, namely that Venetian seems to be primarily a language that is spoken, whereas Friulian is a language one primarily understands. It is a language of which one has passive knowledge. As mentioned above, the subjects of the current paper are not the indigenous residents of Maniago, but the members of the local Albanian speech community. How proficient are they in these languages? Have they learned all three languages? If so, how? Do they consider them important? Do they address others in (one of) these languages? Are (some of) these languages part of their (individual) linguistic repertoire within the Albanian speech community? Have these linguistic varieties in some way modified the (individual) linguistic behavior of these people? And does their use affect the vitality and dominance of the L1? What we, in other words, would like to know is *who speaks what language to whom, when, why, where and what will this lead to* (cf. Fishmann 1970, Berruto 1974 and Candido 2014)?

## 2 Method

### 2.1 *Research Method and Aim*

As indicated in the introduction of this paper, the aim of the present research is to map the linguistic behavior of the L1 Albanian speech community resident in Maniago. In order to give a reliable and broad representation of this behavior, it was decided to use a questionnaire consisting of two parts. A first sociolinguistic part included 80 mainly multiple-choice questions on

A. Personal details, the individual proficiency in various languages and dialects;
B. The migration process;
C. The use of the L1, L2 and other linguistic varieties in everyday life;
D. The distribution of these languages over the several classical and some new (in)formal domains;
E. Personal views on linguistic and cultural integration.

The second part of the questionnaire included 40 Italian sentences of which 50 per cent contained a morphosyntactic deviation, i.e. an interlinguistic interference between standard Italian and another linguistic variety that is believed to be possibly part of the Albanian speech community's linguistic repertoire. The sentences were chosen from three linguistic varieties, namely regional Italian, spoken Italian, and Albanian, famous for their morphosyntactic influence on the standard Italian variety. The first two are not considered identical. We define regional Italian as a spoken variety of Italian that contains grammatical features specific for the north-east of the Peninsula. The term spoken Italian, on the other hand, is used to mark the difference between written and spoken Italian. The linguistic deviation present in the given Italian sentences was chosen with regard to five morphosyntactic subjects:

A. The use of the auxiliary verb *avere* in the perfect tense;
B. Grammatical concordance between the auxiliary verb *essere* and the perfect participle;
C. Phrasal emphasis and word order;
D. The use of articulated prepositions;
E. The phrasal position of the possessive pronouns.

Besides these deviating sentences the list includes sixteen sentences, written in standard Italian, and eight fillers. These last sentences were added to camouflage the aim of the research. In this second part of the questionnaire participants were asked to judge the acceptability of the 48 Italian sentences by choosing one of the five given judgements that varied from acceptable to not acceptable. This acceptability test was inserted in the questionnaire to see if a connection could be found between linguistic behavior and affinity for linguistic varieties.

Before going into the field and using the questionnaire as guideline for the interviews, the correctness and usefulness of its content was analyzed with the help of a pilot test. The questionnaire was presented to and discussed with a number of persons having a high proficiency in both Albanian and Italian, awareness of the linguistic divergence and convergence between the two languages and (most of) its varieties, and knowledge of the social, historical and political context in which migration took place. An adapted version of the questionnaire was used in the period from March until December 2012. All interviews were held in Maniago, in the local library, at the home of the participants or sometimes in one of the bars in the city center. During interviews the questionnaires were in general completed by the researcher, who also had the role of interviewer. Before and/or during the interview participants, obviously, were not informed about the aim of the research. Without detailed explanations, they were asked to answer a number of questions about the language they speak and use in everyday life. Furthermore, they were asked to give their opinion about a list of Italian sentences; it was stressed that there were no correct or incorrect answers. Participants were also informed that participation would be anonymous; the information gathered would be used only for scholarly analysis and for this reason would be treated with absolute discretion.

## 2.2    *Participants*

105 Maniaghese residents expressed a willingness to participate in the research and completed in the questionnaire: 64 mother tongue speakers of Albanian and 41 mother tongue speakers of Italian. The main focus of the research was on the Albanian speaking participants. The Italian speaking participants were primarily important as control group. Their judgment with regard to the acceptability of the sentences and affinity for the Italian language was used to compare the opinion of the Albanian speaking participants. Since a number of sentences contained characteristics of the regional and spoken varieties of Italian, this control group had to consist of Maniaghese inhabitants who not only had Italian as mother tongue, but were born in (the immediate surroundings) of the city and had always lived in the area. This ensured they were aware and/or had developed linguistic skills with regard to the local linguistic repertoire. Furthermore, all participants were at least 18 years old. This last criterion was also applied to the Albanian speaking participants. Of

the 64 Albanian speakers 62 were Albanese and two Kosovan. Together they formed a quarter of the so-called Albanian speech community present in the city of Maniago. Though the aim of the research was to draw a detailed and correct picture of the linguistic behavior of this group and the concern is primarily on the quality of the research, it was considered important to involve as many individuals as possible. Since the participants were found by means of snowball sampling, the actual number of participants that would be found was hard to predict. In addition to the age requirement, a fixed period for searching participants, namely ten months, was established and it was decided that the number of individuals belonging to the control group should not be larger than a quarter of the main group. Turning to the criteria for participation, the Albanian speaking participants should live in (or in the immediate surroundings) of Maniago, have been born in Albania, and have Albanian as first language.

## 2.3　*Data Analysis*

The data based on multiple choice questions was collected in a digital database using Microsoft Excel. Notes, explanations and other useful information given by participants were kept in a different file and, when advisable, consulted to come to a better comprehension and explanation of the results. At a later stage, the multiple-choice data was also entered in another digital database, FileMaker, which made it possible to find answers on more complex research questions requiring a combination of answers to three of more questions.

## 3　Results

### 3.1　*Sociolinguistic Results*

For data analysis, the Albanian mother tongue participants were divided in two groups. Criteria for this division were the participant's age at the moment of migration and the way L2 acquisition took place. These criteria were chosen on the basis of the (socio)linguistic literature (e.g., Bettoni and Rubino 1996; Clyne 2003; Chini 2004).

Basing ourselves on these criteria, two groups were composed. The first one, group A, consisted of 20 participants. These individuals all emigrated to Italy at an early age together with their parents, brothers, sisters and sometimes other relatives; at the time of emigration the youngest were three years and the oldest sixteen. Their first contact with the Italian language was in Italy, where they attended school. These individuals, in other words, learned Italian in an explicit and conscious way. Their language acquisition was of a guided kind.

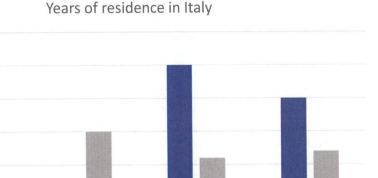

FIGURE 12.3    Years of residence in Italy by group

The 44 Albanian mother tongue speakers grouped in group B, on the other hand, came to Italy having already reached the minimum age of 18; in fact, the average age at immigration was 25. These individuals often migrated together with their family, here partner and children. Generally, their first contact with Italian took place in Albania, where Italian television channels have been available since 1970. Watching these broadcasts, they learned their first words of Italian. After their removal to Italy, all of them drew on this spontaneous, implicit and non-guided way of acquiring the second language.

As shown by Figure 12.3 the majority of the group A members had lived in Italy for more than eleven years. For group B, it is more difficult to define an average number of years of residence, since mutual convergence is high. The majority of all 64 Albanian speaking participants migrated more than ten years ago and they indicated they intended to stay in Italy or even to become Italian citizens. Asking questions with regard to the vitality of the $L_1$ within the speech community, it was found that Albanian still is the language to which most of them feel attached for 50% of group A and 87% of group B. Both interesting and surprising in this context are the results found with regard to the question in what language participants were able to express themselves best. Contrary to expectations, group A members preferred to express themselves in their second language. They indicated this linguistic variety gives them the possibility to express their feelings and thoughts in a more accurate way. Group B members, on the other hand, preferred to use the first language.

This described trend of convergent preference and linguistic behavior was confirmed by the second part of the research. Analyzing the linguistic choices made in several communicative settings, it was concluded that group A members, unlike participants belonging to group B, do not only use the L2 in (in)formal domains in which the interlocutor has no knowledge of Albanian, but also when this language is part of the individual linguistic repertoires of all interlocutors. They, in other words, do not only address colleagues, their boss and/or local shopkeepers in Italian, but also family members, relatives and other Maniaghese residents who have a good proficiency in the Balkan language. In sociolinguistic terms this means that in certain informal domains, originally dominated by the Albanian language, a change has taken place in favor of the host country's language. The mother tongue, in other words, has been replaced by the second language in a great part of the informal domains. There is only one exception: communication with parents most of the time still takes place in the L1, though some group A members declared to sometimes answer their parents' questions in Italian. It will be no surprise that participants of this group indicated to even think, pray and have interior monologues in the second language. The same results were found with regard to the expression of emotions; if this is true, it means that their proficiency in and affinity with Italian has developed to a high level and might even surpass the skills in the L1. Group B members, on the other hand, not only seemed more attached to the first language, but also indicated they expressed themselves better in it, both in monologues and dialogues. Group B members addressed interlocutors who have knowledge of Albanian in this language both in informal and formal domains. It will therefore not come as a surprise that the informal domains are largely dominated by the use of the L1, though some of the participants declared that communication with their children is subject to code switching, as the children introduce new Italian words in the home environment. Most of these Group B members nevertheless keep addressing their children in Albanian. At the same time most formal domains are dominated by the L2. The language choice made by these Maniaghese residents is based on a so-called *matter of need* (cf. Clyne 2003), whereas this choice within in group A seems to be rather the result of a so-called *matter of will*. With the former the choice of a communicative code is based on the individual linguistic repertoire of the other interlocutor. With the latter this choice depends most of all on the personal preference of the speaker.

Besides the so-called classic domains, a number of new domains were included in the questionnaire, namely (social) media. Participants were asked to indicate in what language(s) they search information on the internet, write e-mails and short messages, leave messages on Twitter and Facebook, and/or have Skype conversations. Comparing the answers given by group A and B, far-reaching convergence was found. Information on the internet is always sought in Italian since it concerns everyday life in Italy. The same goes for e-mails, which are used primarily for work-related communication. Furthermore, Twitter was used only by a few participants, so these results were discarded. Texts for short messages and Facebook were written in both Italian and/or Albanian, which also holds for the Skype conversations. With regard to the latter, participants indicated that conversations with relatives and friends living in Albania obviously are in Albanian; the same is true for messages written to individuals living in the Balkan.

On the basis of these results, we believe the linguistic behavior of the group A participants should be described as "dilalia" (cf. Dell'Aquila and Iannàccaro 2004 and 2006). The dominant language, because of its social prestige, is suitable for both formal and informal domains, whereas the subordinate language is only used in (a part of the) informal domains; and its range is reduced by the prestigious language. The linguistic behavior generally found within group B can be defined as multilingualism. Not the type of communicative setting, but most of all the linguistic repertoire of the interlocutor determines language use while interacting with others.

### 3.2   Results of the Acceptability Test

In the second part of the survey, the same division (Group A and Group B) was used to analyze the linguistic results, which were also compared with the answers given by the control group (Group C). Generally, the sentences presented in standard Italian were approved by the majority of the three groups. Particularly the sentences of the following types were identified as being completely acceptable:

A.   The use of the auxiliary verb *avere* in the perfect tense;
B.   Phrasal emphasis and word order;
C.   The phrasal position of the possessive pronouns.

Sentences showing morphosyntactic influence from spoken or regional Italian, like the ones translated from Albanian, evoked more diverse response. In general, groups A and C members tended to judge these sentences negatively. According to these participants the linguistic deviation present in the phrases made them less acceptable; some linguistic expressions were even seen as not acceptable at all. Participants belonging to group B, on the other hand, were quite positive about the same sentences. Although they often identified the linguistic deviation, they did not consider it incorrect.

Interesting in this context are the linguistic proposals made by the members of the three groups. Participants were asked to modify less acceptable phrases on the basis of individual preference. A criterion for these modifications was that the phrasal construction could be changed, but without changing the meaning of the sentence. By giving the participants the possibility to change the original sentences, the reasons for the changes could be ascertained. If the sentence was judged less acceptable participants tended to remove or replace the part of the sentence containing the linguistic deviation. In spite of the divergent judgments, participants of all groups in general tended to change the phrases in this way. Participants, in other words, modified the sentences in a rather economic and simple way. Three sentences, though, could be modified in more than one way. With regard to these sentences, it was noticed that mother tongue speakers of Albanian went for another option than mother tongue speakers of Italian. Without going into details, it was the mother tongue of the participants that informed their decisions. This could usefully be explored in further research.

### 3.3 Conclusion and Discussion

First of all, the *age* on and *stage of life* in which the Albanian speaking participants migrated to Italy seem to have a major effect on their choice of language (cf. Rubino 2003), whereby it should be noted that age and stage do not necessarily coincide. Adolescence is a period in which the influence of the peer group is very strong. Because of their young age at the moment of migration, all group A members experienced this important stage of life in Italy. This emerged during several interviews. The stage of life, in other words, could be one explanation for the difference in linguistic behavior between groups A and B. Participants in group B were living in Albania at this stage. Most of them had already reached another stage of life, for example marriage and/or even parenthood. When they migrated to the peninsula, their identity had already been formed. Their linguistic behavior is characterized by a strong language maintenance that corresponds to the general trend found in different studies. Migration processes that started in a recent past tend to show a high vitality and maintenance of the mother tongue (cf. Rubino 2003). Albanian migration toward Italy started in the early 1990s and up to 2012 five different migration waves were counted. In theory this would mean that the results of the questionnaire show a high dependence on the L1 by the Albanian speech community. As results have demonstrated, this is only partly true, since it holds for group B but not for group A. In order to explain this divergence, we should like to look at the concepts of *context of departure* and *context of arrival* (cf. Romania 2011). Both contexts here put language maintenance at a disadvantage and favor a language shift within the speech community. Albania was a Communist state for almost five decades, from 1946–1990. During this period Albanian citizens were isolated from the rest of the world. When the economic crisis became a threat to the welfare of the population, dissatisfaction grew, especially during the 1970s, when it became possible to watch Italian and Greek television broadcasts and Albanian citizens were able to catch a glimpse of the world outsight the home country. Though it was forbidden to watch foreign television stations, the government was not able to stop the people from doing so. The vicinity of both Greece and Italy simply made it possible to receive the television channels illegally with a satellite dish (cf. Mustafaj 1993). Dissatisfied with their quality of life, people started idolizing the world outside Albania. Once the Communist regime had fallen, many citizens decided to migrate to make their dreams come true. Communist history and its cultural products were collectively rejected. A massive migration process was the consequence. Greece and Italy became favorite destinations. Since the aim of migrating was to start a new and better life abroad, emigrants generally were willing to adapt to the new sociocultural environment. Because of the weak connection between national and religious identity, typical for Communist regimes, Albanian immigrants were quite willing to integrate in the host society. This feeling was further strengthened by the organization of Albanian society. Citizens organize themselves in clans or extended families and interaction between the clans is rare. Albanian speech communities in Italy tend to be organized in the same way. For this reason, Albanian migrants, instead of sticking together, tend to find it easy to make contact with local citizens and other (non-Albanian) individuals living in the host country. Summarizing, it may be said that the context of departure favors a quick language shift.

The same goes for the context of arrival. The Italian government's assimilation politics, for example, does not encourage a vital use of the mother tongue among migrant speech communities, especially when speech community members intend to stay. The role of the Italian press is also very interesting in this context, notably the coverage of the migration process of this specific group of migrants during the 1990s. According to Romania (2011) the above-average speed with which Albanian migrants have adopted the Italian language and culture at the expense of the $L_1$ and $C_1$, springs largely from this press coverage. In March 1991, 25,000 refugees arrived in the harbor of Bari on overcrowded ships. A few months later another 20,000 Albanian migrants arrived in similar conditions. Initially, at that time Italy did not know how to take care of all those people or where to house them. While politicians debated in order to find a suitable solution, the Italian press focused on the fear among the Italian citizens. Migrants, and in particular refugees with the Albanian nationality, where portrayed as criminals and a threat both for the Italian society and its citizens (cf. Bonifazi 2007). Romania (2011) explains that because of this negative image, migrants often tend in some way to camouflage their identity when coming into contact with Italian citizens. This so-called social camouflage of the identity diminishes or removes the chance of being discriminated or judged solely on the basis of identity. By putting on a mask and acting like local residents migrants are able to escape attention. Because of the *contexts of departure* and *arrival*, Albanian migrants are considered masters in camouflaging their original identity. It is even said that their identity is the effect of their performance. Whether this is true or not, a response to press coverage seems to encourage language shift, rather than language maintenance. In fact, research results show that both in group A and B the vitality of the mother tongue is decreasing. Group B members with children indicate that, although they address their children in Albanian only, the children tend to respond in Italian. These participants say they regret this linguistic choice of their children, although they do accept it. Participants belonging to group A, on the other hand, indicate they have consciously chosen Italian as language of communication for their family; even when their partner originates from Albania, their children are raised in Italian. The vitality of the L1 within the next generation, in other words, is likely to decrease even more. A complete language shift in one or two generations seems inevitable. It would be very interesting for future research to follow this new, Italian-born generation and map their linguistic behavior, combining sociolinguistic theories with intercultural communication. Though most varieties belonging to the Maniaghese linguistic repertoire seem to have had little influence on the language choices of the respondents, this might not be true for next generations.

## References

Berruto, Gaetano. *La sociolinguistica*. Bologna: Zanichelli, 1974.

Bettoni, Camilla, and Antonia Rubino. *Emigrazione e comportamento linguistico; un'indagine sul trilinguismo dei siciliani e dei veneti in Australia*. Galatina: Congedo, 1996.

Bonifazi, Corrado. *L'immigrazione straniera in Italia*. Bologna: Il Mulino, 2007.

Candido, Elisa. "Vivere il plurilinguismo; la comunità albanofona nel comune di Maniago." Dissertation, Università degli Studi di Udine, 2014.

Chini Marina. *Plurilinguismo e immigrazione in Italia. Un'indagine sociolinguistica a Pavia e Torino*. Milano: Francoangeli, 2004.

Clyne, Michael. *Dynamics of language contact*. Cambridge: Cambridge University Press, 2003.

Dell'Aquila, Vittorio, and Gabrielle Iannàccaro. *La pianificazione linguistica. Lingue, società e istituzioni*. Rome: Carocci, 2004.

Dell'Aquila, Vittorio, and Gabrielle Iannàccaro. *Survey Ladins. Usi linguistici nelle valli Ladine*. Trento: Regione Autonoma Trentino Alto-Adige, 2006.

Devole, Rando. *L'immigrazione albanese in Italia; dati, riflessioni, emozioni*. Rome: Agrilavoro edizioni, 2006.

Francescato, Giuseppe. "Il confine occidentale dell'area friulana: alcune cosiderazioni." In *Nuovi studi linguistici sul friulano*, edited by Giuseppe Francescato, 17–47. Udine: Società Filologica Friulana, 1991.

Francescato, Giuseppe. "Il friulano a Maniago: due vitalità a confront." In *Nuovi studi linguistici sul friulano*, edited by Giuseppe Francescato, 55–91. Udine: Società Filologica Friulana, 1991.

Manzelli, Gianguido. "Italiano e albanese: affinità e contrasti." In *Italiano e lingue immigrate a confronto: riflessioni per la pratica didattica*, edited by Chiara Ghezzi, 151–196. Perugia: Guerra, 2004.

Mustafaj, Besnik. *Albania: tra crimini e miraggi*. Milano: Grazanti, 1993.

Orioles, Vicenzo. *Le minoranze linguistiche; profili sociolinguistici e quadro dei documenti di tutela*. Rome: Il Calamo, 2003.

Picco, Linda. *Ricercje su la condizion sociolenghistiche dal furlan*. Udine: Forum, 2011.

Romania, Vicenzo. *Farsi passare per italiani; strategie di mimetismo sociale*. Rome: Carocci, 2011.

Rubino, Antonia. "Prospettive di mantenimento linguistico: fase di vita e di comunità come fattori di variabilità tra gli italiani in Australia." In *Ecologia linguistica. Atti del XXXVI congresso internazionale di studi della Società di Linguistica Italiana (SLI). Bergamo 26–28 settembre 2002*, edited by Ada Valentini, 309–329. Roma: Bulzoni, 2003.

Triolo, Riccardo. *L'allievo di origine albanese*. Cestim centro studi immigrazione, 2006. www.cestim.it.

CHAPTER 13

# The Impact of Bilingual Education on Written Language Development of Turkish-German Students' L2

*Esin Işıl Gülbeyaz*

1     Introduction

In 2001, the Program for International Student Assessment (PISA) identified a close correlation between social background and deficits in equal opportunities in Germany: children from socially disadvantaged families scored significantly below their better-off classmates (Stanat et al. 2010, 225). Although the influence of social background on educational achievement has decreased in Germany, it remains high in comparison to other countries (German Federal Ministry of Education and Research—BMBF 2019).

Given the importance of written language skills and multilingualism in school, higher education and other social environments, the present study examines two overarching questions:

(a)   at what level of complexity do Turkish-German bilingual students at secondary levels I and II write or, more specifically, which type of compound and complex sentences do they use when writing argumentative texts in their two languages?

(b)   how much does the first-language input in the school context influence the written language development of students in their two languages?

To answer these questions, written expository texts from Turkish-German bilingual students in the 7th, 10th, and 12th grades in their first language Turkish (L1) and in their second language German (L2) are examined, using texts from bilingual students from two different schools. It is important to underline that all students whose texts are analyzed in this study are Turkish-German bilingual students. To investigate the impact of the schooling type (bilingual vs. monolingual), i.e. the type and intensity of L1 instruction on bilingual students' written language development (research question (b) above), these students were divided into two groups. The first group of bilingual students used Turkish as their first language and as a language of instruction in a Turkish-German bilingual setting (pupils with TU1); the second group of bilingual students used Turkish as their second foreign language from 7th grade in a German monolingual setting (pupils with TU7). The data was collected by the MULTILIT[1] project of the University of Potsdam, funded by the German Research Association *Deutsche Forschungsgesellschaft* (DFG) and its French partner organisation *L'Agence nationale de la recherche* (ANR).

The present paper focuses on the bilingual students' expository texts, written in German. The theoretical part (1) reviews the presentation of Maas' concept of language enhancement, *Sprachausbau*, (Maas 2010), which was chosen as theoretical framework for this study. The first section (1) gives an overview of Maas' model and presents differences between his model of syntactic complexity and its adaptation in this study. The empirical part (2) begins with explanations of the research questions, the students' profile, the data corpus and the method (2.1). Section 2.2, Data Evaluation, gives detailed information on the sentence types, the norm violations or deviations investigated here, and on the perspective from which these are interpreted in the present study.

## 2  Theoretical Framework

The theoretical framework for the analysis of this study is Maas' (2010) concept of language enhancement (*Sprachausbau*), which is concerned with the gradual development of written language competence. This gradual development is seen as a continuum between orate and literate structures, i.e., between informal and formal language use. Maas' concept of language enhancement has parallels with Cummins' BICS-CALP[2] differentiation (Cummins 1980; Cummins and Swain 1986) although Maas does not mention them (for a detailed discussion of these parallels, see Gülbeyaz 2020). In brief, Cummins (1980; Cummins and Swain 1986) and Maas (2010) integrate elements of register differentiation into their theoretical models. In addition to the existing parallels, a fundamental difference between the theoretical models of Cummins (1980; Cummins and Swain 1986) and Maas (2010) should be pointed out here, which is relevant for the selection of Maas' model as the theoretical framework in the present study. This difference concerns the fact that in Cummins' (1980; Cummins and Swain 1986) model the criteria by which the respective developmental stages

---

1  Development of Oral and Written Abilities in L1, L2 and L3 by Multilingual Children and Adolescents with Turkish Background in France and German. https://www.uni-potsdam.de/de/daf/projekte/multilit [5.1.2021].
2  BICS refers to Basic Interpersonal Communication Skills, CALP to Cognitive Academic Language Proficiency.

between the two ends of a continuum, from informal (context-embedded) to formal (context-reduced) communication, can be identified and analysed remain unclear, whereas Maas (2010) defines the developmental stages in terms of syntactic complexity using syntactic structures. There are a number of reasons for using Maas' model here, the first being its focus on form, or syntax, which overlaps with the purpose of this study; on the other hand, according to his sentence definition, sentences can be divided into propositions, i.e. sub-sentences, which allows for syntactic analysis with the corpus linguistic software EXMARaLDA.[3] Moreover, Maas' structuring of language enhancement into stages of acquisition with corresponding syntactic constructions can be productively applied to the research question about the syntactic complexity of sentences in written texts. This is especially the case as Maas' (2010) model for language enhancement is designed to be crosslinguistic and can be adapted to Turkish and German in this study, in line with the research question. Finally, due to the classification of certain syntactic structures as orate or literate, Maas' (2010) model, which is conceived in a cross-formal and crosslinguistic way, provides an analytical tool for formal analyses such as the one conducted in the present research. On each level of the syntactic complexity scale, the syntactically simple sentence becomes progressively more enhanced (language enhancement), which Maas (2010, 92) classifies as follows:

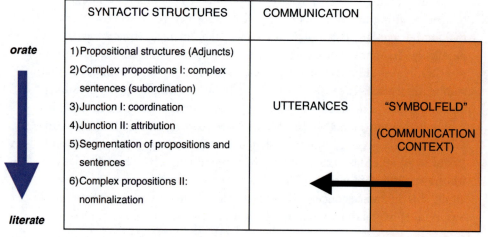

FIGURE 13.1  Maas' model of language enhancement: orate to literate continuum
MAAS 2010: 92, TRANSLATED BY THE AUTHOR

---

3   Extensible Markup Language for Discourse Annotation.

According to Maas' model of written language development (Figure 13.1 above) an utterance understood by the other person ensures successful communication. However, this does not mean that this utterance is literate, i.e. syntactically complex. An utterance is literate if it is fully articulated (a sentence) by the *Symbolfeld*, i.e. in a given communication context. An enhanced form of utterance would be a text whose literate level is determined by its decomposability into sentences or by its structure in sentences (Maas 2010, 92). In Figure 13.1 above, the further enhanced forms of a syntactically simple sentence according to Maas are presented. The literate character of an utterance, i.e. a sentence, goes hand in hand with the degree of syntactic complexity of the enhancement. If the enhancement is more complex than that of a syntactically simple sentence, it is more literate (Maas 2010, 92). The following examples from Maas exemplify the categories in Maas' model (Figure 13.1 above) and explain his idea of a scalar development of written language skills at the syntactic level. The examples are presented together with the corresponding category in Maas' model. Maas' model is approached critically, however (for further details see Gülbeyaz 2020). As a result its application to the languages studied here, Turkish and German, also includes some variation. Below differences are explained on the basis of Maas' examples:

(1) Propositional structures (adjuncts)
   (a) "*Letzte Woche* ging Emma mit ihrem Dackel spazieren."[4]
   (Emma went for a walk with her dachshund *last week*.);
   (b) "*Vor einer Woche* ging Emma mit ihrem Hund spazieren."
   (Emma went for a walk with her dog *a week ago*.)
   (c) "*Es war (passierte) letzte Woche*, dass Emma mit ihrem Dackel spazieren ging."
   (It was (happened) last week, that Emma went for a walk with her dachshund.)

The adverbial adjuncts such as "*letzte Woche*" (last week) in (a) (see above) or "*vor einer Woche*" (a week ago) in (b) are not the focus of the present study, which centers on compound and complex sentences introduced by cohesive devices such as conjunctions, e.g., *und* (and), and subjunctions, e.g. *obwohl* (although) (difference nr. 1). Furthermore a sentence like (c) is considered in this study according to its syntactic structure as a (main) sentence "*Es war*

---

4 The examples (a) to (j) are from Maas (2010, 84 ff.) and translated by the author. The order of the examples varies in this paper.

(*passierte*) *letzte Woche*" (It was (happened) last week) whose subject "*es*" (it) is specified, modified, by a complement clause "*dass Emma mit ihrem Dackel spazieren ging*" (that Emma went for a walk with her dachshund) (difference nr. 2).

(2) Complex propositions I: complex sentences (subordination)
    (d) "Daß Hans ihr Blumen schenkt, gefällt Emma."
        (That Hans gives her flowers, pleases Emma.)
    (e) "Als Hans mit dem Dackel spazieren ging, schlief Emma."
        (When Hans went for a walk with the dachshund, Emma was sleeping.)

(3) Junction I: coordination
    (f) "Hans kam nach Hause und Emma legte sich ins Bett."
        (Hans came home and Emma went to bed.)

In Maas' complexity scale, sentences like (d) are considered less literate than coordinated sentences like (f). In the study presented in this paper coordinated clauses (f) are considered less literate than complement clauses as in (d) (difference nr. 3) which are followed by adverbial clauses as in (e) on the complexity scale developed by the author (see Figure 13.2 below) (difference nr. 4).

(4) Junction II: attribution

Maas (2010) classifies adverbial attributes modifying the verb or predicate such as "*müde*" (tired) in (g) and "*schwarz*" (black) (h) under this category of attribution (4), together with the attributes modifying nouns such as the adjective "*müde*" (tired) in (i) and such as the relative clause "*der fürchterlich müde war*" (who was terribly tired) in (j).

    (g) "Hans kam **müde** nach Hause."
        (Hans came home **tired**.)
    (h) "Emma trinkt ihren Kaffee **schwarz**."
        (Emma drinks her coffee **black**.)
    (i) "Der **müde** Hans wurde wieder munter, als er Emma sah."
        (Hans, who was **tired**, became lively again when he saw Emma.)
    (j) "Hans, **der fürchterlich müde war**, wurde munter, als er Emma sah."
        (Hans, **who was terribly tired**, became lively when he saw Emma.)

At this point, the question arises why the sentences (g) and (h) each containing, syntactically, only a simple adverb and without any propositional enhancement such as subordination or a complex nominal phrase, should be more complex than the sentences enhanced by complement clauses in examples (c) and (d) above or the sentence expanded by an adverbial clause in (e). Syntactically simple sentences, i.e. not enhanced by either a subordination or a complex nominal phrase, such as in (g) and (h) are categorized in the present study as simple sentences, representing the first, most orate level of enhancement on the complexity scale developed by the author (see Figure 13.2 in section 2) (difference nr. 5). Maas (2010), in contrast, considers such sentences as more enhanced (complex) than coordinated sentences such as (f) and subordinated complement or adverbial clauses such as (c), (d) and (e) above. Adjectival attributes as in (i) are analyzed in this study only when they occur together with a participle attribute such as *der müde und erschöpfte Man*[5] (the tired and exhausted man) (difference nr. 6), since syntactic structures enhanced by participle attributes as well as by subordination such as the relative clause in (j) are the focus of the linguistic analysis explained in the empirical part (section 2) below.

(5)   Segmentation of propositions and sentences

In this study, following Maas (2010, 88), a proposition has a predicate as the 'head.' Thus compound and subordinated sentences are considered as propositions here: *Ich würde dieses Buch gern lessen, weil ich es interessant finde*[6] (I would like to read this book because I find it interesting) is a complex sentence, consisting of a main sentence *Ich würde dieses Buch gern lessen* (I would like to read this book) and of a proposition which is, in this example, a subordinated sentence or subordination *weil ich es interessant finde* (because I find it interesting). Segmentation of propositions and sentences, to determine the boundaries of propositions and sentences, is unlike in Maas' model not part of the syntactic complexity scale developed as a category grid for the analysis of written language development by Gülbeyaz (2020) (see Figure 13.2 in section 2.2 below). This category grid includes only syntactic structures, in the present study simple, compound and complex sentences, whereas the question about the segmentation of propositions and sentences is considered here

---

5   Maas' example modified by the author.
6   Example given by the author. The author's examples are highlighted through italic font, quoted examples through italic font and quotation marks "...".

as an essential methodological criterion for the (corpus)linguistic analysis that is to be conducted before applying the category grid to the data corpus (difference nr. 7). Therefore, to investigate the type of sentences in written texts, we have to determine first what we consider as a sentence (its beginning and end) and which role propositions play as part of sentences.

(6) Complex propositions II: nominalization

Since the basis of syntactic analysis in the present study is syntactic integration (of information) through (complex) sentences, nominalizations are analyzed here only when they occur together with a participle attribute such as *die erwartete Genehmigung* (the expected authorisation) (difference nr. 8). This procedure follows from the fact that a participle attribute has a sentence-like character since it is decomposable into a subordination, e.g. attributive clause such as the relative clause *die erwartet wurde* (that was expected) in the following example: *die Genehmigung, die erwartet wurde* (the authorisation that was expected).

In the above critical presentation of Maas' model, it becomes clear that the syntactic enhancement in written language proceeds from simple sentence to nominalization (Maas 2010, 92; see also Augst and Faigel 1986, 78; Feilke 1996, 1182; Feilke 1993, 9), in the words of Augst and Faigel (1986) and Feilke (1996; 1993) "from the sequential to the integrative." "Sequential" refers to enhancement of a sentence through coordinations or subordinations, whereas "integrative" is related to enhancement of a nominal phrase through participle or genitive attributes, for example. This means that in written language information is "packaged" (Chafe 1982, 39) or expressed in an increasingly language-economic, efficient and compact way. Maas (2010, 92) defines this increase in informative content of a syntactic structure (sentence or nominal phrase) through sequence or integration as *"Informationsverdichtung"* (information density) and, similar to Augst and Faigel (1986) and Feilke (1996; 1993),[7] considers integration on the nominal phrase level as the highest level of written language acquisition.

In the model of language enhancement adapted here by the author (see Figure 13.2 in section 2), syntactic complexity in the form of enhanced (complex) sentences in both languages, Turkish and German, is assigned to a developmental stage of written language acquisition, ranging from orate to literate

---

[7] Maas (2010) does not mention Augst and Faigel (1986) and Feilke (1996; 1993) nor the parallels with their work.

structures. Mastery of literate structures demonstrates the learner's development towards a higher level of syntactic complexity in written language.

## 3 Empirical Part

### 3.1 Research Questions and Methodology

Because of the importance of written language skills and multilingualism in school and social contexts, the present study explores the overarching questions:

(a) what is the complexity level of the writing of Turkish-German bilingual students in lower and upper secondary schools and what type of literate structures, i.e. enhanced (compound and complex) sentences do they use when writing argumentative texts in their two languages?

(b) to what extent do the type and intensity of first-language instruction in the school context (bilingual vs. monolingual setting) influence students' written language development in their two languages?

To answer these questions, written expository texts in Turkish (L1) and German (L2) by Turkish-German bilingual students from the 7th, 10th, and 12th grades were examined. Students from two different schools in Berlin participated in the research. For the first group Turkish was used as the language of instruction from 1st grade in a Turkish-German bilingual setting (students with TU1), while in the second group Turkish was used as a language of instruction from 7th grade as a foreign language in a German monolingual (students with TU7). Five students were selected per class. This resulted in 30 students and a total of 60 texts (30 texts per language). The general selection criterion for both groups of students was that the subjects were born in Germany, with one exception, and all were schooled in Germany. Students from the bilingual secondary school received Turkish-German bilingual education from first grade according to the school's concept. The subjects from the German monolingual secondary school started Turkish classes in 7th grade. The purpose of these criteria was to form groups that were as homogeneous and comparable as possible with regard to the different Turkish instruction in both schools.

From a quantitative point of view, the number of participants is fairly low, which is caused by the above selection criteria, as well as by the fact that there are few schools in Germany that offer bilingual education, especially when the other language is a (low-prestige) migration language as it is the case for Turkish in Germany.

Due to the manageable data corpus as well as the mixed research approach used here to analyze the data not only quantitatively but also qualitatively, no statistically significant results were aimed for. Rather, the aim was not only to quantify the linguistic structures used by the subjects, but to use the quantitative analysis to provide an overview of the type and frequency of constructions used by the students. As a next step, conspicuous features of the quantitative results will be discussed below in more detail in a qualitative analysis, taking into account factors such as family and personal motivation for education, access to media, language choice for media and oral as well as written contexts.

### 3.2 A Category Grid for Syntactic Analysis of Written Language Development in German as Second Language

To understand the syntactic development of bilingual students from 7th to 12th grade in German as a second language, the following sentence structures of German were analyzed. The examples below as well as in section 2.3 are taken from the corpus investigated here, from Turkish-German bilingual secondary level students' written texts. The examples are presented without any correction of norm violations or deviations occurring in the original students' texts.

Syntactic structures of German analyzed in this study:

(1) Simple clause (syntactically not complex/not enhanced)
AYL_10_TU7
"*Natürlich finde ich Streit nicht so gut.*"
'Of course I don't like fights.'

(2) Coordination through coordinative conjunctions within a sentence
OSM_10_TU1
"*Es sind zwar schlechte Sachen **aber** es gehört zum Schulleben.*"
'These are bad things, **but** they are a part of school life.'

(3) Subordination
  (a) Complement clause (introduced by subjunctions such as *dass-* (that), *ob-* (whether), question words and infinitive construction)
  GOEK_10_TU7 (complement clause introduced by *dass* (that))
  "*Ich denke, [**dass** man reden muss], wenn man Probleme lösen will.*"
  'I think [**that** one has to talk] if one wants to solve problems.'
  ZEH_7_TU1 (complement clause introduced by *wie* (how))
  "*Ich denke, dass wir das Film geckugt haben, damit wir verstehen [**wie** wir uns gegenseitig in der Schule behandeln]*."

'I think that we watched the film so we can understand [**how** we treat each other mutually at school].'

EDA_7_TU7 (complement clause introduced by a *zu* (to)+*infinitive* construction)

"*Es war eigendlich ein Fehler von dem Mädchen [das Geld einzustecken] [...]."*

'It was actually a mistake on the part of the girl [**to pocket** the money] [...].'

(b) Adverbial clause

EDA_7_TU7 (Causal clause introduced by *weil* (because))

"*Alles im Ganzen hat der Film mir gefallen, [weil er mir gezeigt hat] wie auch ander Kinder sein können.*"

'Overall I liked the film [**because** it showed me] how other children can be.'

(c) Attributive clause

EMI_12_TU1 (Relative clause introduced by a.o. *der/die/das* (that))

"*Im Kurzfilm wurden Situationen erzählt, [die man jederzeit im Alltag erlebt].*"

'In the short film, situations were narrated [**that** one experiences at any time in everyday life].'

EMI_12_TU1 (Attributive complement clause introduced by *dass* (that))

"*Die negativen Seiten (wären)*[8] *die Konsequenzen, [dass man mit 0 Punkten bestraft wird], wenn man erwischt wurde.*"

'The negative sides would be the consequences [**that** one would get penalized with 0 points] if he/she gets caught.'

(4) Participle construction

YAL_12_TU7

"*[Der Ausgegrenzte Schüler /-in] fühlt sich oft alleine und ist hoffnungslos und unbeholfen.*"

'The pupil **excluded/rejected** (by his/her classmates) often feels lonely and is hopeless and helpless.'

For a better overview, the categories shown above can be represented in a category grid as follows:

---

8  The student has crossed out the predicate "wären (would be)" in her/his text, probably in the course of a self-correction or rewording.

| Level of syntactic complexity | Turkish | German |
|---|---|---|
| orate | 1. Simple clause (finite) | 1. Simple clause (finite) |
| | 2. Coordination through coordinative conjunctions, e.g. *ve* (and), within a sentence (finite) | 2. Coordination through coordinative conjunctions, e.g. *und* (and), within a sentence (finite) |
| | 3. Subordination (predominantly infinite) | 3. Subordination (predominantly finite) |
| | a) Complement clause (introduced by suffixes or infixes *-mAK, -mA* and *-DIK/-(y)AcAK-*) (infinite) | a) Complement clause (introduced by *dass-* (that), *ob-* (whether), question words (finite) and infinitive constructions (infinite)) |
| | b) Adverbial clause (predominantly infinite) | b) Adverbial clause (predominantly infinite) |
| | | c) Attributive clause (introduced by relative pronouns *dass-* (that), *ob* (whether), question words (finite) and infinitive constructions (infinite)) |
| literate | b) Participle construction / attributive clause (introduced by the suffixes or infixes *-DIK-* und *-(y)An-*) (infinite) | 4. Participle construction / participle attribute (infinite) |

FIGURE 13.2  Category grid for syntactic analysis of written language development in Turkish and German
GÜLBEYAZ 2020, 170

This complexity scale for both languages presented in the category grid (Figure 13.2) was developed by Gülbeyaz (2020) for syntactic analysis of written language development in Turkish and German. Similar to Maas (2010, 87), the basis of syntactic analysis in the present study is "syntactic integration." Although the underlying idea of a syntactic complexity scale for literate structures in written language is based on Maas' model of language enhancement (Maas 2010), as presented above, there are several important differences between the Gülbeyaz' and Maas' model. An additional distinction between the two models emerges from the fact that Gülbeyaz' model is designed for Turkish and German, while taking into account the typological differences between the two languages.

The following section (2.3) presents the results of the quantitative as well as qualitative analysis of texts written by bilingual students in secondary school. As in the previous sections, the focus will be on texts written in German. Nonetheless, in order to refer to the impact of bilingual education on written language development in L1 and L2, at appropriate points also results regarding the Turkish texts will be mentioned.

## 3.3 *Results of Quantitative and Qualitative Analyses of German Texts*

The results of the quantitative analysis show that both the Turkish-German bilingually and German monolingually schooled groups of bilingual students use literate structures such as complex subordinations more frequently with increasing age in both languages. This development shows similarities with monolingual (written) language acquisition. However, the two groups differ from each other in that the bilingually schooled group (with TU1) uses simple and compound sentences, both considered orate structures, less frequently over time than the monolingually schooled group (with TU7). The group with TU1 instead uses complex sentences more often. Furthermore, the same bilingually schooled group uses highly literate structures, i.e. complex sentences such as attributive clauses, earlier than the monolingually schooled group does. This result is closely related to Cummins' 'Interdependence Hypothesis' (1979; 2000), according to which pupils who are educated bilingually in their family language and second language are more successful in terms of cognitive and academic development than bilingual pupils who are educated monolingually in their second language. These students achieve a lower level of written language proficiency, called "literacy" by Cummins:

> Many bilingual students experience academic failure and low levels of literacy in both their languages when they are submersed in an L2-only instructional environment; however, bilingual students who continue to develop both languages in the school context appear to experience positive cognitive and academic outcomes.
> 2000, 174

Qualitative analysis gives detailed insight in sentences bilingual secondary school students use frequently or rarely. Furthermore, it helps identify difficulties that become visible when the students try to use syntactically complex sentences, which are likely to be new in their linguistic repertory. In the present study, qualitative analysis produced the following results. In the German texts, in the category of subordinations, in both groups complement clauses are most frequently used, followed by adverbial clauses (see category and example 3 (b) in Gülbeyaz' model, section 2.2 above) and attributive clauses (category and example 3 (c) (i)). Participle constructions such as "*dein Leben prägende Dinge*" (things **shaping** your life) and "*nach einer vergangenen Klausur*" (after a **past** exam) are rarely used by both groups: participle structures occur sporadically and only in 12th grade, once in the group with TU1 and three times in the group with TU7.

The two groups differ from each other in that the group with TU1, in the developmental span from 7th to 12th grade, increasingly uses in their L1 Turkish and their L2 German significantly more attributive clauses, mainly relative clauses (see category and example 3 (c) (i) in Gülbeyaz' model in 2.2 above), than the group with TU7 (see also Gülbeyaz 2020, 193; 2017: 128). Consequently, the increase in attributive clauses, especially relative clauses, in the corpus analyzed here also supports Maas' (2010, 106, 112) assumption that enhanced nominal groups (complex nominal phrases) as well as relative clauses are relatively more frequent in written than in spoken language. On the other hand, this finding refutes, where English is concerned, Biber and Clark's (2002, 46), Biber et al.'s (1999, 8) and, for German, Siekmeyer's (2013, 73) statements about a complex relative clause being mainly more frequent in spoken language than in written language. Since in the corpus analyzed here the use of relative clauses increases over time, the author of this study assumes that for the age groups investigated here, between 7th and 12th grade, linguistic abilities to form and frequently use relative clauses are not a given, but are acquired by the students over time. That is, as students' writing skills improve, more attributive clauses can be expected in their texts. Given the fact that participle constructions occur sporadically in the students' texts and only in 12th grade, i.e., less frequently and at a later stage than relative clauses, Gülbeyaz (2020, 194) assumes that attributive clauses, and especially relative clauses, are possibly a precursor to participle constructions. Furthermore, according to the Interdependence Hypothesis (Cummins 2000, 174), a more frequent use of highly literate attributive clauses (category 3 (c) in Figure 13.2 above) by students with TU1 could be attributed to the positive influence of their bilingual schooling, in their L1 Turkish as well as in their L2 German.

Another important finding of this study with regard to high frequency structures is that in both groups, complement clauses by means of *dass* (that) (category and example 3 (a) (i) in Gülbeyaz' model in section 2.2 above) and complement clauses by means of *zu-infinitive* (to + infinitive) (category and example 3 (a) (iii)) are the most frequent complement clause types. Finally, with regard to rarely or never occurring structures, it should be noted that their underrepresentation or absence in student texts should not be directly attributed to the fact that students do not master these constructions well and therefore try to avoid them or that they do not have them in their linguistic repertoire. One reason for the underrepresentation or absence of certain constructions in student texts may be that such complex linguistic structures with high information density are learned later and solidified over time, just like the participle constructions in this corpus, which occur sporadically and only in 12th grade. Another reason may be that students find certain structures unsuitable for the register in which they have to speak or write, as may be the case with complement clauses by means of *ob* (whether) (category 3 (a) in Figure 13.2 in section 2.2) as well as with the asyndetic and therefore informal subordination type SVO (Subject-Verb-Object) in German texts. It may also simply be that the writing occasion and what the student wants to tell or write does not trigger the use of certain constructions, as might be the case with respect to complement clauses introduced by *ob* (whether), attributive complement clauses by means of *dass* (that), and attributive complement clauses *zu-Infinitiv* (to + infinitive) in this corpus.

Another important finding of this study is related to norm violations or deviations. In this text, the term 'deviations' is used uniquely to evaluate the data from a language development point of view. In this context both groups of students show an increase in norm deviations in both morphology and syntax in the Turkish and German texts from 7th to 12th grade. The fact that norm deviations are more frequent in both groups in grade 12 than before could possibly be attributed, among other factors, to the fact that students produce increasingly longer texts in the time period between grade 7 and grade 12 and that the syntactic complexity of sentences increases. Furthermore, the analysis of norm deviations shows that the German monolingually schooled bilingual students (with TU7) have more frequent norm deviations in the areas of morphology and syntax in both their languages than the Turkish-German bilingually schooled group of bilingual students (with TU1) (see also Gülbeyaz 2020; 2017, 128). This result allows us to assume that, due to the influence of bilingual schooling, the group with TU1 has fewer norm deviations in morphology and syntax in both languages than the group with TU7.

## 4 Conclusion

The results of this study show that, with increasing age, both the Turkish-German bilingually and German monolingually schooled groups of bilingual pupils use complex sentences more frequently in both languages, similar to monolingual language acquisition. However, the two groups differ from each other in that the bilingually schooled group (with TU1) uses orate structures such as simple and compound sentences (orate structures) less frequently over time than the monolingually schooled group (with TU7), and instead uses complex sentences such as different types of subordinations more often. Additionally, the bilingually schooled group also shows fewer errors and norm deviations in morphological and syntactic areas, especially in Turkish, but also in German. These results indicate that family language instruction provides expanded access to literate structures in both languages and affects the (academic) writing skills in second language positively in terms of more frequent and earlier use of literate structures such as attributive clauses and fewer norm deviations in writing contexts. The comparison of the two groups also demonstrates that written language acquisition requires school instruction of the first language(s) to be integrated into the official curriculum (see also Herkenrath 2012).

## References

Augst, Gerhard, and Peter Faigel. *Von der Reihung zur Gestaltung. Untersuchungen zur Ontogenese der schriftsprachlichen Fähigkeiten von 12–23 Jahren*. Frankfurt am Main: Peter Lang, 1986.

Biber, Douglas, and Victoria Clark. "Historical Shifts in Modification Patterns with Complex Noun phrase Structures. How Long Can You Go without a Verb?" in *English Historical Syntax and Morphology*, edited by Teresa Fanego, Javier Pérez-Guerra and María José López-Cuoso, 43–66. Amsterdam: John Benjamins Publishing Company, 2002.

Biber, Douglas, Stig Johansson, Geoffrey Leech, Susan Conrad, and Edward Finegan. *Longman Grammar of Spoken and Written English*. London: Longman, 1999.

*Bildung im Schulalter*. BMBF, Bundesministerium für Bildung und Forschung, 2019. Accessed April 14, 2019. https://www.bmbf.de/de/pisa-programme-for-international-student-assessment-81.html.

Chafe, Wallace. "Integration and Involvement in Speaking, Writing, and Oral Literature." In *Spoken and Written Language: Exploring Orality and Literacy*, edited by Deborah Tannen, 35–53. Norwood, NJ: Ablex, 1982.

Cummins, Jim. *Language, Power and Pedagogy. Bilingual Children in Crossfire. Bilingual Education and Bilingualism 23.* Clevedon/Buffalo/Toronto/Sydney: Multilingual Matters Ltd, 2000.

Cummins, Jim, and Merrill Swain. *Bilingualism in Education. Aspects of Theory, Research and Practice. Applied Linguistics and Language Study.* London/New York: Longman, 1986.

Cummins, Jim. "The Cross-Lingual Dimensions of Language Proficiency: Implications for Bilingual Education and the Optimal Age issue." *TESOL Quarterly* 14 (1980): 175–187.

Cummins, Jim. "Linguistic Interdependence and the Educational Development of Bilingual Children." In *Bilingual Education Paper Series* 49, no. 2 (1979): 222–251.

Diehl, Erika, Helen Christen, Sandra Leuenberger, Isabelle Pelvat, and Thérèse Studer. *Grammatikunterricht, alles für der Katz? Untersuchungen zum Zweitsprachenerwerb Deutsch.* Tübingen: Niemeyer 2000.

Kunkel-Razum, Kathrin. *Duden, die Grammatik unentbehrlich für richtiges Deutsch.* Mannheim/Leipzig/Wien/Zürich: Duden Verlag, 2005.

EXMARaLDA. Ein Teilprojekt „Computergestützte Erfassungs- und Analysemethoden multilingualer Daten" des Sonderforschungsbereichs „Mehrsprachigkeit" (SFB 538) der Universität Hamburg. Accessed April 30, 2019. https://exmaralda.org/de/ueber-exmaralda/.

Feilke, Helmuth. "Schreibentwicklungsforschung. Ein kurzer Überblick unter besonderer Berücksichtigung der Entwicklung prozessorientierter Schreibfähigkeiten." *Diskussion Deutsch* 129 (1993): 17–34.

Feilke, Helmuth. "Die Entwicklung der Schreibfähigkeiten." In *Schrift und Schriftlichkeit—Writing and Its Use. Band 2*, edited by Harmut Günther and Otto Ludwig, 1178–1191. Berlin: De Gruyter, 1996.

Herkenrath, Annette. "Receptive Multilingualism in an Immigrant Constellation: Examples from Turkish-German Children's Language." *International Journal of Bilingualism* 16, no. 3 (2012): pp. 287–314.

Maas, Utz. "Literat und orat. Grundbegriffe der Analyse geschriebener und gesprochener Sprache." *Grazer Linguistische Studien* 73 (2010): 21–150.

Gülbeyaz, Esin Işıl. *Schriftspracherwerb und Mehrsprachigkeit. Syntaktische Komplexität bei Satzverknüpfungsverfahren mehrsprachiger Schülerinnen und Schüler in ihrer Erst- und Zweitsprache. Mehrsprachigkeit/Multilingualism series* 50. Münster/New York/München/Berlin: Waxmann, 2020.

Gülbeyaz, Esin Işıl. "Syntaktische Komplexität bei Satzverknüpfungsverfahren mehrsprachiger SchülerInnen in ihrer Erst- und Zweitsprache—Untersucht anhand schriftlicher argumentativer Texte türkisch-deutsch mehrsprachiger SchülerInnen." In: *Mehrsprachigkeit: Spracherwerb, Unterrichtsprozesse, Seiteneinstieg*, edited by Isabel Fuchs, Stefan Jeuk, Werner Knapp, 111–135. Stuttgart: Fillibach bei Klett, 2017.

Herkenrath, Annette. "Receptive Multilingualism in an Immigrant Constellation: Examples from Turkish-German children's Language." *International Journal of Bilingualism* 16, no. 3 (2012): 287–314.

MULTILIT, research project at the University of Potsdam. Accessed on January 5, 2021. https://www.uni-potsdam.de/de/daf/projekte/multilit.

Sieber, Peter, and Sitta Horst. "Sprachwandel—Sprachfähigkeiten." In *Sprachfähigkeiten—Besser als ihr Ruf und nötiger denn je!*, edited by Peter Sieber, 13–50. Aarau/Frankfurt am Main/Salzburg: Sauerländer, 1994.

Siekmeyer, Anne. "Sprachlicher Ausbau in gesprochenen und geschriebenen Texten Zum Gebrauch komplexer Nominalphrasen als Merkmale literater Strukturen bei Jugendlichen mit Deutsch als Erst- und Zweitsprache in verschiedenen Schulformen." Dissertation, Saarland University, 2013. Accessed January 31, 2021. http://dx.doi.org/10.22028/D291-23626.

Stanat, Petra, Dominique Rauch and Michael Segeritz. "Schülerinnen und Schüler mit Migrationshintergrund." In *PISA 2009. Bilanz nach einem Jahrzehnt,* edited by Eckhard Klieme, Cordula Artelt, Johannes Hartig, Nina Jude, Olaf Köller, Manfred Prenzel, Wolfgang Schneider, and Petra Stanat, 200–230. Münster: Waxmann, 2010.

CHAPTER 14

# Linguistic Advantages of Bilingualism: The Acquisition of Dutch Pronominal Gender

*Elena Tribushinina and Pim Mak*

1    Introduction

Bilingualism has often been associated with delays in language development. Bilinguals usually have smaller vocabularies than their monolingual peers in each language (Bialystok et al. 2010; Pearson et al. 1993) and may develop their languages at a slower pace (Unsworth 2013). Furthermore, bilingual children sometimes make errors under the influence of the other language. For example, French-English bilinguals sometimes incorrectly place English adjectives after the nouns (as in French), which results in erroneous noun-phrases such as 'the mouse mad' (Nicoladis 2006). This phenomenon is known as negative cross-language transfer.

However, evidence is accumulating that acquisition of two languages may also have a positive influence on child development. For instance, the famous 'bilingual advantage' in cognitive development refers to the recurrent finding that bilinguals have enhanced executive functions (Bialystok 1988, 2010). In contrast, relatively little attention has been paid to *linguistic* advantages of bilingualism. Bilingual children have knowledge of two language systems, and these two systems interact in a bilingual mind. If a particular category is acquired early in one of the languages, its development in the other language can be accelerated (Armon-Lotem 2010). This phenomenon is known as "positive transfer" or "bilingual bootstrapping" (Gawlitzek-Maiwald and Tracy 1996). According to the bilingual bootstrapping hypothesis, "something that has been acquired in language A fulfills a booster function for language B" (Gawlitzek-Maiwald and Tracy 1996, 903). For example, longitudinal case studies have revealed that Cantonese-English bilinguals may acquire the Cantonese progressive aspect marker *gan* faster than their monolingual peers, presumably due to the early acquisition of the progressive construction in their other language (English) (Luk and Shirai 2018). Similarly, English-Spanish bilinguals appear to acquire the English copula *be* earlier than English-speaking monolinguals (Fuertes and Liceras 2010). English toddlers often omit the copula in locative constructions (e.g., 'Mary is in the garden') or in sentences denoting temporary states (e.g., 'Mary is ill'). English-Spanish bilinguals are less likely to omit copulas in these constructions, probably because Spanish has two copulas corresponding to the English 'be' (*ser* and *estar*), the latter being used specifically to predicate transient locations and states.

The present paper will contribute to the relatively scarce literature investigating the workings of positive transfer in a bilingual mind. Until now it is not clear whether bilingual bootstrapping requires typological proximity between the two languages. Furthermore, no study thus far has directly compared the effects of positive transfer in bilinguals acquiring two languages from birth (simultaneous bilinguals) and child second language learners (early sequential bilinguals). This paper will do just this and compare the production of pronominal gender by monolingual Dutch-speaking children and Russian-Dutch (both simultaneous and early sequential) bilinguals.

The paper is structured as follows. Section 2 briefly discusses prior research on the acquisition of grammatical gender in general and Dutch gender in particular. Section 3 explains the set-up of this study and presents the hypotheses that will be tested in the experiments reported in Sections 4 and 5. Section 6 presents a general discussion and conclusions from this research.

## 2 Theoretical Background

### 2.1 *The Acquisition of Grammatical Gender*

The ability to distinguish biological gender, that is, the distinction between males and females, is generally acquired quite early, usually by age 2.5 (Fagot, Leinbach and Hagan 1986). Grammatical gender is more complex and is usually acquired later. As far as transparency and salience of gender systems is concerned, there are large typological differences between languages, and these typological properties affect the rate of acquisition. Languages such as Spanish, Italian, Russian, Greek and Hebrew offer their learners multiple cues for gender assignment. Besides semantic cues (e.g., biological gender), children acquiring these languages can rely on noun-internal (morphophonological) cues and noun-external (agreement) cues. Noun-internal cues involve predictability of gender based on the noun ending. For example, Russian masculine nouns usually end in a consonant (e.g., *telefon* 'telephone'), most feminine nouns end in *-a* (e.g., *obezjana* 'monkey'), and neuter nouns end in *-o/-e* (e.g., *moloko* 'milk,' *serdce* 'heart'). Noun-external cues involve agreement with other elements in the sentence. For instance, Russian nouns display gender agreement with adjectives (both attributive and predicative), demonstrative pronouns, possessive pronouns and past-tense verb forms.

Such transparent gender systems are acquired very early, usually before the age of 4 (Belacchi and Cubelli 2012; Berman 1985; Gathercole 2002; Gvozdev 1961; Lew-Williams and Fernald 2007; Rodina 2008). In contrast, the acquisition of non-transparent gender systems, such as grammatical gender in Dutch, Norwegian and Welsh, is known to be a difficult and protracted process (De Houwer and Gillis 1998; Hulk and Cornips 2006; Rodina and Westergaard 2013; 2017; Thomas and Gathercole 2007). In these languages children still make errors at age 9. Fhlanntchadha and Hickey (2017) have found that Irish-English bilinguals are still far from complete acquisition of the opaque gender system of Irish, even at age 13 and even after formal schooling in Irish.

The vast majority of studies on the acquisition of grammatical gender deal with gender agreement in the attributive domain (marked on determiners and adjectives). Relatively little is known about the acquisition of pronominal gender. Mills (1986) reports that English-speaking preschoolers aged 3–4 correctly apply 'it' to inanimate referents, but tend to over-generalize 'he' to all animate referents. However, English-speaking children are already sensitive to gender cues in sentence processing by age 4 (Arnold, Brown-Schmidt and Trueswell 2007).

## 2.2   The Acquisition of Dutch Gender

Dutch marks two genders (common and neuter) in the attributive domain and has a three-way gender system (masculine, feminine, neuter) in the pronominal domain. In Belgian Dutch, the choice of a pronoun is determined by the grammatical gender of the antecedent, whereas in Netherlandic Dutch (focus of the present study) gender agreement in the pronominal domain is mainly based on semantic principles (Audring 2009). Masculine pronouns are used with reference to human males, but also inanimate referents that are bounded and countable (e.g., table). Feminine pronouns are used exclusively for human and (less commonly) animal females. For example, an individual fish would usually be referred to as *hij* 'he,' unless it is a cartoon fish which is conspicuously female (e.g., Dory from the movie *Finding Nemo* is referred to as *zij* 'she'). Finally, the neuter pronoun *het* 'it' is used for unbounded and uncountable inanimates (e.g., fish as a dish).

Dutch gender marking is opaque and notoriously difficult to acquire (Blom, Polišenská and Weerman, 2008; Blom and Vasic 2011; De Houwer and Gillis 1998; Keij et al. 2012; Orgassa and Weerman, 2008; Unsworth 2008; Unsworth et al., 2014). In the attributive domain a child can only use two cues for gender assignment: the definite determiner in the singular (*de* for common gender and *het* for neuter) and the unmarked form of attributive adjectives combined with singular, neuter, indefinite nouns (in all other cases attributive adjectives end in *-e*). Not surprisingly, Dutch-speaking children still frequently make gender agreement errors, even after age 7 (Brouwer, Sprenger and Unsworth 2017; Hulk and Cornips, 2006). For example, Unsworth et al. (2014) report that 6-six-year-old Greek-English bilinguals are at ceiling performance with gender markings on determiners (in Greek), whereas Dutch-English bilinguals of the same age are only 36% correct with the neuter determiner (in Dutch).

This said, Cornips and Hulk (2006) have shown that bidialectal children growing up with standard Dutch and the Heerlen dialect acquire the gender distinction in Dutch much faster than monolingual Dutch-speaking children. In Heerlen Dutch there is a three-way gender system that is morphologically visible on definite and indefinite determiners and hence is more salient and transparent than in standard Dutch. Cornips and Hulk (2006) suggest that considerable structural overlap between the gender systems of Dutch and Heerlen Dutch leads to positive transfer and facilitates acquisition. The present paper pursues the question whether positive transfer in the gender domain is also possible between languages that are less typologically similar and have very different gender systems (Netherlandic Dutch and Russian). Recent findings reported by Egger, Hulk and Tsimpli (2018) and Kaltsa, Tsimpli and Argyri (2019) suggest that positive transfer between typologically distant languages should be possible.

This study also extends this line of research to gender agreement between the pronoun and its antecedent. Whereas the acquisition of grammatical gender in the attributive domain has received a great deal of attention in the literature, much less is known about the acquisition of gender in the pronominal domain. Children acquiring languages where pronoun choice is determined by noun gender (German, Belgian Dutch) usually acquire basic principles of gender agreement in the pronominal domain by age 5, but still make errors at age 7–8 (De Vogelaer 2006; Mills 1986). Hulk and Cornips (2010) tentatively conclude that children acquiring Netherlandic Dutch learn to apply the pronoun *het* correctly (i.e., with reference to inanimate uncountable referents) by age 5. We do not know, however, when the distinction between masculine and feminine pronouns is acquired in Netherlandic Dutch. Mills (1986) reports that English-speaking 4-year-olds over-generalize *he* to female referents. Likewise, anecdotal evidence suggests that Dutch-speaking children attending primary school overuse the masculine pronoun *hij* 'he' for female referents. This observation will be tested in the experiments reported below.

## 3   This Study

The present study compares pronoun use in the narratives produced by Dutch-speaking monolinguals and their bilingual Russian-Dutch peers. Since Netherlandic Dutch does not mark biological gender grammatically outside the pronominal domain, children receive little evidence of feminine versus masculine gender marking. Hence, we expect this aspect of pronoun use to be problematic to all groups of children acquiring Dutch. However, bilingual children acquiring Dutch along with Russian are expected to perform better than their monolingual peers, since the acquisition of Dutch pronoun gender by these children might be supported by their knowledge of Russian. As explained above, Russian has a transparent system of gender assignment. Gender agreement is amply marked on verbs, adjectives and other attributes (relative/demonstrative pronouns, numerals, etc.). Pronoun choice in the singular is determined by the grammatical gender of the antecedent. Only in some exceptional cases is it determined by the biological gender of the referent (e.g., *papa* 'dad' is grammatically feminine, but should agree with masculine pronouns, verbs and modifiers). Due to the salience and transparency of Russian grammatical gender, gender assignment and gender agreement in Russian are acquired already by age 3–4 (Gvozdev 1961). Thus, bilingual Russian-Dutch preschoolers have already learnt that the masculine-feminine distinction is relevant in Russian, which may channel their attention towards a similar distinction in Dutch and thereby facilitate acquisition.

This paper reports two experiments. Experiment 1 compares pronoun use by 7-year-old Dutch-speaking monolinguals and two groups of bilingual children—simultaneous bilinguals acquiring Dutch and Russian from birth (2L1) and early sequential bilinguals (eL2) whose first language (L1) is Russian and second language (L2) is Dutch. Based on Mills (1986), we hypothesize that monolingual children will overuse masculine pronouns. Bilingual children are expected to use more feminine pronouns than monolinguals. Since eL2 children have had more exposure to Russian, the extent of crosslinguistic influence from Russian is likely to be larger for this group. Finally, two adult groups were included in the study: (a) L1 Dutch speakers and (b) L2 speakers of Dutch with L1 Russian. The inclusion of the L1 adult group was necessary in order to establish a baseline of target-like performance. Since gender agreement with pronouns is driven by semantic principles rather than grammatical rules, we can only speak of adult-like patterns of use rather than analyze the results in terms of accuracy. The adult L2 participants were all mothers raising their children bilingual in the Netherlands. They all spoke Russian to the children and Dutch to their spouses. Hence, their narratives provide an indication of pronoun use in the non-native Dutch input provided by Russian-speaking parents in mixed families.

Experiment 2 targets pronoun use by younger children (age range 4–6) in order to establish whether the effects of crosslinguistic influence, if any, are stronger at an earlier age (cf. Argyri and Sorace 2007; Hulk and Müller 2000).

## 4   Experiment 1

### 4.1   *Method*

#### 4.1.1    Participants

Fifty-six children participated in the experiment, including 20 monolingual (L1) Dutch-speaking children (mean age: 7;9), 20 simultaneous (2L1) bilingual Russian-Dutch children (mean age: 7;8) and 16 early sequential (eL2) bilinguals (mean age: 8;0). All participants lived in the Netherlands. L1 children were recruited from a primary school in Utrecht, 2L1 children from Russian weekend schools in Amsterdam, Hilversum and Amersfoort, and eL2 children from the Russian weekend school in Eindhoven.

The 2L1 children were born in the Netherlands and were raised bilingual from birth, in most cases by a Russian mother and a Dutch father. They attended a regular Dutch school from age 4 onwards and a Russian complementary school during the weekend.

The eL2 children were born in Russia; their first exposure to Dutch was around age 4. They spoke Russian at home (with both parents) and Dutch outside the home. Like the 2L1 participants, they attended a regular Dutch school during the week and a Russian complementary school on Saturday.

There were also 45 adult participants: 30 L1 speakers of Dutch and 15 L1 Russian L2 Dutch speakers. The L2 group were parents of bilingual children in the Netherlands (but not necessarily of the children participating in this experiment). They all spoke Russian to their children and Dutch to their spouses. Their first exposure to Dutch was in adulthood, upon immigration to the Netherlands.

#### 4.1.2    Materials and Procedure

Two sets of six pictures were used to elicit narratives: the Fox Story (Gülzow and Gagarina 2007) and the Cat Story (Hickmann 2003). These narratives were selected because their protagonists (cat, dog and bird in the Cat Story; fox, bird and fish in the Fox Story) are all labelled by feminine nouns in Russian. This creates a context in which crosslinguistic influence is likely to occur. The pictures were simple black-and-white drawings.

Narrative collection was part of a larger study (see the Discourse BiSLI corpus in the CHILDES archive, Tribushinina, Dubinkina and Sanders 2015; Tribushinina et al. 2017). In this project, bilinguals produced one narrative in Russian and one in Dutch (either Cat or Fox). Each language was tested in a separate session, by a native speaker of Russian and Dutch, respectively. The order of tasks/languages was counterbalanced among the participants. Only Dutch narratives were included in the present study. The monolingual participants were randomly assigned to one of the narratives (Cat or Fox) to ensure the comparability of the samples.

The children were interviewed individually in a quiet room in their school. The adults were tested in their homes. The participant was sitting in front of the investigator. The six-picture set was first placed on the table (in two rows of three pictures) and the participant was asked to look through the pictures and confirm that (s)he has understood the plot. After that the investigator removed the pictures from the table and started presenting them one by one. The most recent picture was always kept in sight so that the participant could link the two pictures in a narrative.

The narratives were audio-recorded and transcribed in a CHAT format (Mac-Whinney 2000). Only singular masculine and singular feminine pronouns were targeted for analysis. The following pronominal forms were included in the counts: personal pronouns in the nominative case (*hij/ie* 'he,' *zij/ze* 'she'), personal pronouns in the accusative (*hem* 'him,' *haar* 'her') and possessive pronouns (*zijn* 'his,' *haar* 'her'). All ambiguous cases, where the antecedent of the pronoun could not be unambiguously established, were excluded from analysis. Repetitions and self-corrections were also excluded from further consideration.

## 4.2 Results

Figure 14.1 presents the percentage of masculine pronouns used in the narratives of each group. Note that all nouns referring to the protagonists are feminine in Russian.

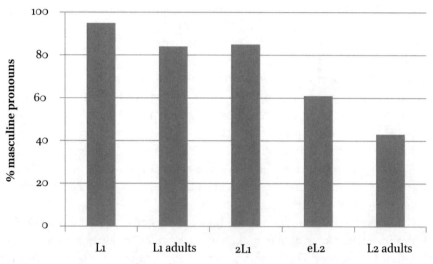

FIGURE 14.1   Percentage of masculine pronouns, by group

The data were analyzed using logistic regression in R (Bates et al. 2015). We tested whether (and how) the groups differed in the probability of producing a masculine pronoun. L1 adults were used as the baseline. The model coefficients are presented in Table 14.1

TABLE 14.1   Coefficients of the comparisons between groups

|  | B | SE | z value | p value |
| --- | --- | --- | --- | --- |
| Intercept (L1 adults) | 1.65 | 0.29 | 5.66 | < .001 |
| 2L1 children | 0.05 | 0.40 | 0.13 | 0.89 |
| L2 adults | −1.95 | 0.37 | −5.30 | < .001 |
| eL2 children | −1.21 | 0.38 | −3.17 | 0.002 |
| L1 children | 1.09 | 0.51 | 2.13 | 0.03 |

As can be seen in Table 14.1, only the simultaneous bilingual group (2L1) did not differ from the L1 adults in the probability of using masculine pronouns.

Monolingual children barely used feminine pronouns and produced significantly more masculine pronouns than L1 adults. In contrast, both L2 groups produced significantly more feminine forms than L1 adults. An analysis taking L2 adults as a reference group shows that they produced significantly more feminine forms than eL2 children, $B = 0.74$, $SE = 0.33$, $z = 2.21$, $p = .03$.

A closer scrutiny of pronoun use for each protagonist reveals that the participants were most likely to use feminine pronouns when speaking about the mother-bird (Cat Story). L2 adults used only feminine pronouns with reference to this protagonist, eL2 children and L1 adults used more feminine than masculine pronouns, 2L1 children used almost equal numbers of feminine and masculine pronouns, and L1 children used more masculine than feminine forms.

Another character that attracted feminine pronouns was the fox. Both L2 groups used more feminine than masculine pronouns for this protagonist. Simultaneous bilinguals preferred masculine pronouns, but also used feminine forms. L1 children and adults never used feminine pronouns for the fox.

Interestingly, with reference to the cat bilingual children (both eL2 and 2L1) were equally likely to use masculine and feminine pronouns, unlike L2 adults, who exclusively used masculine pronouns. L2 adults in their turn preferred feminine pronouns for reference to the bird from the Fox Story; all other groups used masculine pronouns for this character. The fish (Fox Story) and the dog (Cat Story) were never referred to by means of feminine pronouns, not even by the L2 groups.

### 4.3  Discussion

The results of this experiment have revealed that at age 7 only simultaneous bilinguals display the adult-like pattern of pronoun use. 2L1 children overwhelmingly use masculine pronouns, but tend to apply both masculine and feminine forms to the conspicuously female character (mother-bird). Monolingual children of this age use masculine pronouns, even with reference to the mother-bird. This finding seems to support the hypothesis that crosslinguistic influence from a gender-rich language may facilitate the acquisition of Dutch pronominal gender by bilinguals. At the same time, like L2 participants but unlike L1 adults, the 2L1 children sometimes used feminine pronouns with reference to the fox, which suggests that there is not only positive but also negative transfer from Russian.

The results reported above are compatible with the idea that the differences between L1 and 2L1 children are due to the interaction of the gender systems in a bilingual mind. In this scenario bilingual participants use more feminine forms because gender systems of Dutch and Russian influence each other. However, we cannot rule out the possibility that bilinguals produced more feminine forms because they were exposed to feminine pronouns in the non-native Dutch input from their Russian mothers. As evidenced by Figure 14.1 Russian adults use more feminine than masculine pronouns in their L2 narratives. They are especially likely to use feminine forms with reference to protagonists that are often featured as females in Russian fairy-tales (fox, bird). Notice in this connection that even though the noun *sobaka* 'dog' is grammatically feminine and agrees with a feminine pronoun in Russian, dogs are more often males in Russian folklore. This might explain why all participants, including the Russian-speaking adults, used only masculine pronouns with reference to the dog.

We have also found an interesting difference between 2L1 children and L2 adults. Like eL2 children, but unlike L2 adults, simultaneous bilinguals sometimes used feminine pronouns to refer to the cat. The reason might be that there are two words for 'cat' in Russian (*koška*-FEM and *kot*-MASC). The absence of feminine references to the cat in the adult L2 data may indicate that crosslinguistic influence from Russian might still be a relevant factor, along with non-native input.

The data in Figure 14.1 suggest that the use of feminine forms is related to exposure to Russian. Russian-speaking adults were raised and educated in Russian. L2 children started off with Russian, but are currently growing up in a dominant Dutch environment and attend regular Dutch schools. 2L1 children have had much more exposure to Dutch than to Russian. The proportions of feminine pronouns in the speech of these three groups neatly reflect these patterns of exposure and dominance.

In this experiment we have targeted pronoun use by relatively old children. It is often assumed in the literature that crosslinguistic influence abates with age, as children become more proficient in their languages (Argyri and Sorace 2007; Hulk and Müller 2000). In order to determine whether there is more crosslinguistic influence under age 7, Experiment 2 compared pronoun use by younger bilingual children (aged 4–6) and their monolingual peers. Only simultaneous bilinguals were included in this experiment.

## 5 Experiment 2

### 5.1 Method

#### 5.1.1 Participants

One hundred fifty-one children participated in this experiment: 77 Dutch-speaking monolinguals and 74 Russian-Dutch simultaneous bilinguals. The children were between 4 and 6 years of age. The bilingual participants (17 four-year-olds, 28 five-year-olds, 29 six-year-olds) were born in the Netherlands; they attended a Dutch primary school during the week and a Russian-language school/kindergarten at the weekend. The bilingual participants were recruited through the Russian schools in Amsterdam, Amersfoort, Hilversum and The Hague. The monolingual participants (26 four-year-olds, 26 five-year-olds, 25 six-year-olds) were recruited through regular primary schools in North-Brabant.

### 5.1.2   Materials and Procedure
The materials and procedure were identical to those in Experiment 1.

## 5.2   *Results*
The frequencies of feminine pronouns were very low in both groups: 1% in the monolingual group (N=218) and 10% in the bilingual group (N=270). In the monolingual group, feminine pronouns were attested only in the narratives of two 4-year-old children (one feminine pronoun in each narrative). Four-year-old bilinguals did not use feminine pronouns, but a small number of 5-year-olds and 6-year-olds did. In total, 11 bilingual children used a feminine pronoun at least once. Hence, the data did not allow for a logistic regression analysis. Instead, we performed a chi-square test on the number of children who used at least one feminine pronoun in their narratives. The results show that the proportion of children using feminine pronouns is higher in the bilingual group: $\chi^2$ (1) = 7.22, $p$ = .007. The proportion of children using feminine pronouns in the group of 5-6-year-old bilinguals is not significantly different from the proportion of feminine pronoun users in the 7-year-old bilingual group (Experiment 1): $\chi^2$ (1) = 1.02, $p$ = .31.

A closer look at pronoun use per referent shows that 2L1 children, like L1 adults in Experiment 1, used feminine pronouns to refer to the mother-bird. Unlike L1 adults, they occasionally used feminine pronouns with reference to the fox and the bird (Fox Story).

## 5.3   *Discussion*
As in Experiment 1, bilinguals used more feminine pronouns than monolinguals, however only from age 5 onwards. So our hypothesis that crosslinguistic influence abates with age is not borne out by the data. On the contrary, bilingual children come to use more feminine forms with age, presumably as a function of growing proficiency in Russian. But again, we do not know whether the differences between monolinguals and bilinguals are due to crosslinguistic influence as such or due to input effects.

## 6  General Discussion and Conclusion

This study tested the prediction of the bilingual bootstrapping hypothesis that Russian-Dutch bilinguals may have an advantage over their monolingual Dutch-speaking peers in the acquisition of pronoun gender. Since both gender assignment and gender agreement in Russian are salient and transparent, bilingual children may be more sensitive to gender cues in Dutch compared to monolingual peers. The results reported above are compatible with this hypothesis. Simultaneous bilinguals use feminine pronouns as often as Dutch-speaking adults, particularly with respect to the mother-bird in the Cat Story. In contrast, monolingual Dutch-speaking children barely use feminine pronouns, not even with reference to the conspicuously female character (cf. Mills 1986). In this respect, bilingual children indeed seem to have an advantage over their monolingual peers. Hence, for positive transfer to take place, language systems do not even have to be typologically or structurally similar (as in Cornips and Hulk 2006). Positive transfer is also possible between typologically different languages (cf. Egger et al. 2018; Luk and Shirai 2018). In this respect it is noteworthy that the pronominal gender systems in Dutch and Russian are governed by fundamentally different principles: Dutch pronominal gender is based on semantic principles, whereas pronominalization in Russian is by and large governed by the grammatical gender of the noun.

This said, we also see evidence of negative transfer from Russian. There are cases in which adult monolingual speakers of Dutch (and L1 children) do not use feminine pronouns, but simultaneous bilinguals and L2 speakers do (e.g., referring to the fox and to the cat).

How can the attested differences between monolinguals and bilinguals be explained? One possibility is that the Russian system with its more salient gender cues influences the Dutch system in the bilingual mind (learner-internal explanation). An alternative (learner-external) explanation is that 2L1 children hear feminine pronouns in the non-native Dutch input provided by their mothers in conversations with non-Russian-speaking family members. As shown by the results of Experiment 1, adult Russian speakers of L2 Dutch use more feminine than masculine pronouns in their narratives, which indicates that bilingual children probably hear quite some feminine pronouns in the input. In a similar fashion, Cornips and Hulk (2006) argue that non-native input from L2 parents of ethnic minority children might at least partly explain these children's non-target-like production of gender markers in the attributive domain.

At the same time, the differences between 2L1 and eL2 children in the prevalence of feminine pronouns suggest that learner-internal factors also play a role, since the attested differences reflect the children's exposure to Russian. 2L1 children usually speak Russian only with their mother and at the Russian weekend school. Child L2 learners were exclusively exposed to Russian during the first years of life and continue speaking Russian at home (which makes the language-external explanation less plausible for this group). It is possible that greater experience with Russian makes Russian gender more accessible and hence more difficult to inhibit, which explains a higher transfer rate in the eL2 group. Notice also that the use of feminine forms by 2L1 children increases with age. It seems likely that developing proficiency in Russian is positively related to (positive and negative) transfer from Russian. The finding that children with greater exposure to Russian use more feminine forms in Dutch is consonant with the idea of crosslinguistic influence inside the bilingual processing system.

In summary, bilinguals use more feminine pronouns than monolingual speakers and the proportion of feminine pronouns in their speech increases as a function of age and exposure to Russian (L2 adults > eL2 children > 2L1 children). However, based on the current data, we cannot determine whether this crosslinguistic influence originates in the mind of a bilingual learner or comes in the ready-made form from the non-native input. In future studies, it would be useful to collect information on the participants' cumulative exposure to and proficiency in each language in order to correlate these measures with the ratio of feminine pronouns in their speech. Another promising direction for future research would be to pinpoint the quantity and quality of non-native input for each child and to relate these variables to the child's pronoun production (e.g., by testing mother-child dyads). If feminine forms in child speech stem primarily from non-native input, there should be a positive relation between pronoun use by the mother and by the child. If, however, the child's own experience with and proficiency in Russian prove to be the primary predictors of pronoun use, this might indicate that learner-internal transfer mechanisms play a greater role. It is also plausible that both learner-internal and learner-external factors contribute to the pattern of pronoun use attested in this study. Future research will be crucial to resolving this issue.

## Acknowledgements

We would like to thank all children, teachers and parents who made this investigation possible. This research was supported by a Marie Curie IRSES Fellowship within the 7th European Community Framework Programme (grant number 269173).

## References

Argyri, Efrosyni, and Antonella Sorace. "Crosslinguistic Influence and Language Dominance in Older Bilingual Children." *Bilingualism: Language and Cognition* 10, no. 1 (2007): 79–99.

Armon-Lotem, Sharon. "Instructive Bilingualism: Can Bilingual Children with Specific Language Impairment Rely on One Language in Learning a Second One?" *Applied Psycholinguistics* 31, no. 2 (2010): 253–260.

Arnold, Jennifer, Sarah Brown-Schmidt, and John Trueswell. "Children's Use of Gender and Order-of-Mention during Pronoun Comprehension." *Language and Cognitive Processes* 22, no. 4 (2007): 527–565.

Audring, Jenny. "Gender Assignment and Gender Agreement." *Morphology* 18 (2009): 93–116.

Bates, D., M. Maechler, and B. Bolker. "Lme4: Linear Mixed-Effects Models Using S4 Classes (R package version 0.999999-2)." *Journal of Statistical Software* 67, no. 1 (2013): 1–48. http://CRAN.R-project.org/package=lme4.

Belacchi, Carmen, and Roberto Cubelli. "Implicit Knowledge of Grammatical Gender in Preschool Children." *Journal of Psycholinguistic Research* 41, no. 4 (2012): 295–310.

Berman, Ruth. "The Acquisition of Hebrew." In *The Crosslinguistic Study of Language Acquisition, Vol. 1: The Data*, edited by Dan Slobin, 255–373. Hillsdale, NJ: Lawrence Erlbaum Associates, 1985.

Bialystok, Ellen, Gigi Luk, Kathleen F. Peets, and Sujin Yang. "Receptive Vocabulary Differences in Monolingual and Bilingual children." *Bilingualism: Language and Cognition* 13, no. 4 (2010): 525–531.

Bialystok, Ellen. "Global-Local and Trail-making Tasks by Monolingual and bilingual Children: beyond Inhibition." *Developmental Psychology* 46, no. 1 (2010): 93–105.

Bialystok, Ellen. "Levels of Bilingualism and Levels of Linguistic Awareness." *Developmental Psychology* 24, no. 4 (1988): 560–567.

Blom, Elma, and Nada Vasic. "The Production and Processing of Determiner-noun Agreement in Child L2 Dutch." *Linguistic Approaches to Bilingualism* 1, no. 3 (2011): 265–290.

Blom, Elma, Daniela Polišenská, and Fred Weerman. "Articles, Adjectives and Age of Onset: The Acquisition of Dutch Grammatical Gender." *Second Language Research* 24, no. 3 (2008): 289–323.

Brouwer, Susanne, Simone Sprenger, and Sharon Unsworth. "Processing Grammatical Gender in Dutch: Evidence from Eye Movements." *Journal of Experimental Child Psychology* 159 (2017): 50–65.

Cornips, Leonie, and Aafke Hulk. "External and Internal Factors in Bilingual and Bidialectal Language Development: Grammatical Gender of the Dutch Definite Determiner." In *L2 Acquisition and Creole Genesis*, edited by Claire Lefebvre, Lidia White and Christine Jourdan, 355–378. Amsterdam/Philadelphia: Benjamins, 2006.

De Vogelaer, Gunther. "Pronominaal genus bij 'Zuid-Nederlandse' taalverwervers: Van grammaticaal naar semantisch systeem." In *Nederlands tussen Duits en Engels*, edited by Matthias Hüning, Ulrike Vogl, Ton Van der Wouden and Arie Verhagen, 89–102. Leiden: Stichting Neerlandistiek Leiden, 2006.

Egger, Evelyn, Aafke Hulk, and Ianthi Maria Tsimpli. "Crosslinguistic Influence in the Discovery of Gender: The Case of Greek-Dutch Bilingual Children." *Bilingualism: Language and Cognition* 21, no. 4 (2018): 694–709.

Fagot, Beverly I., Mary D. Leinbach, and Richard Hagan. "Gender Labeling and the Adoption of Sex-typed Behaviors." *Developmental Psychology* 22, no. 4 (1986): 440–443.

Fhlannchadha, Siobhan Nic, and Tina M. Hickey. "Acquiring an Opaque Gender System in Irish, an Endangered Indigenous Language." *First Language* 37, no. 5 (2017): 475–499.

Fuertes, Raquel Fernández, and Juana Muños-Liceras. "Copula Omission in the English Developing Grammar of English/Spanish Bilingual Children." *International Journal of Bilingual Education and Bilingualism* 13, no. 5 (2010): 525–551.

Gathercole, Virginia C.M. "Grammatical Gender in Bilingual and Monolingual Children: A Spanish Morphosyntactic Distinction." In *Language and Literacy in Bilingual Children*, edited by D. Kimbrough Oller, and Rebecca E. Eilers, 207–219. Clevedon: Multilingual Matters, 2002.

Gawlitzek-Maiwald, Ira, and Rosemary Tracy. "Bilingual Bootstrapping." *Linguistics* 34, no. 5 (1996): 901–926.

Gillis, Steven, and Annick de Houwer. *The Acquisition of Dutch*. Amsterdam: Benjamins, 1998.

Gülzow, Insa, and Natalia Gagarina. "Noun Phrases, Pronouns and Anaphoric Reference in Young Children Narratives." In *Intersentential Pronominal Reference in Child and Adult Language*, edited by Dagmar Bittner and Natalia Gagarina, 203–223. Berlin: ZAS Papers in Linguistics, 2007.

Gvozdev, A.N. *Formirovanie u rebeka grammatičeskogo stroja russkogo jazyka* [Language development of a Russian child]. Moscow: APN RSFSR, 1961.

Hickmann, Maya. *Children's Discourse. Person, Space, and Time across Languages*. Cambridge: Cambridge University Press, 2003.

Hulk, Aafke, and L. Cornips. "Neuter Gender and Interface Vulnerability in Child L2/2L1 Dutch." In *Paths of Development in L1 and L2 Acquisition*, edited by Sharon Unsworth, Teresa Parodi, Antonella Sorace and Martha Young-Scholten, 107–134. Amsterdam/Philadelphia: Benjamins, 2006.

Hulk, Aafke, and L. Cornips. "The Role of Gender and Count Features in the Acquisition of 'het' as a Pronoun: Similarities and Differences with Its Acquisition as a Determiner." In *Language Acquisition and Development: Proceedings of GALA 2009*, edited by Joao Costa, Ana Castro, Maria Lobo and Fernanda Pratas, 229–239. Newcastle: Cambridge Scholars, 2010.

Hulk, Aafke, and N. Müller. "Crosslinguistic Influence in Bilingual Children: Object Omission and Root Infinitives." In *Proceedings of the 24th Annual BU Conference on Language Development*, edited by Catherine Howell, Sarah A. Fish and Thea Keith-Lucas, 546–557. Sommerville, MA: Cascadilla Press, 2000.

Kaltsa, Maria, Ianthi Maria Tsimpli, and Froso Argyri. "The Development of Gender Assignment and Agreement in English-Greek and German-Greek Bilingual Children." *Linguistic Approaches to Bilingualism* 9, no. 2 (2019): 253–288.

Keij, Brigitta, L. Cornips, Roeland Van Hout, Aafke Hulk, and Joanne Van Emmerik. "The Acquisition of Grammatical Gender and the Definite Determiner in Dutch by L1-TD, L1-SLI, and eL2 children." *Linguistic Approaches to Bilingualism* 2, no. 4 (2012): 379–403.

Lew-Williams, Casay, and Anne Fernald. "Young Children Learning Spanish Make Rapid Use of Grammatical Gender in Spoken Word Recognition." *Psychological Science* 18, no. 3 (2007): 193–198.

Luk, Zoe Pei-sui, and Yasuhiro Shirai. "The Development of Aspectual Marking in Cantonese-English Bilingual Children." *International Review of Applied Linguistics in Language Teaching* 56, no. 2 (2018): 1–43.

MacWhinney, Brian. *The CHILDES Project: Tools for Analyzing Talk*. Mahwah, NJ: Lawrence Erlbaum Association, 2000.

Mills, Anne E. *The Acquisition of Gender a Study of English and German*. Berlin: Springer-Verlag, 1986.

Nicoladis, Elena. "Cross-linguistic Transfer in Adjective-noun Strings by Preschool Bilingual Children." *Bilingualism: Language and Cognition* 9, no. 1 (2006): 15–32.

Orgassa, Antje, and Fred Weerman. "Dutch Gender in Specific Language Impairment and Second Language Acquisition." *Second Language Research* 24, no. 3 (2008): 333–364.

Pearson, Barbara, Sylvia C. Fernández, and D. Kimbrough Oller. "Lexical Development in Bilingual Infants and Toddlers: Comparison to Monolingual Norms." *Language Learning* 43, no. 1 (1993): 93–120.

Rodina, Yulia, and Marit Westergaard. "Grammatical Gender in Bilingual Norwegian–Russian Acquisition: The Role of Input and Transparency." *Bilingualism: Language and Cognition* 20, no. 1 (2017): 197–214.

Rodina, Yulia, and Marit Westergaard. "The Acquisition of Gender and Declension Class in a Non-transparent System: Monolinguals and Bilinguals." *Studia Linguistica* 67 (2013): 47–67.

Rodina, Yulia. "Semantics and Morphology: The Acquisition of Grammatical Gender in Russian." Dissertation, University of Tromsø, 2008.

Thomas, Enli M., and Virginia C. Mueller Gathercole. "Children's Productive Command of Grammatical Gender and Mutation in Welsh: An Alternative to Rule-based Learning." *First Language* 27 (2007): 251–278.

Tribushinina, Elena, Elena Dubinkina, and Ted Sanders. "Can Connective Use Differentiate between Children with and without Specific Language Impairment?" *First Language* 35, no. 1 (2015): 3–26.

Tribushinina, Elena, Willem M. Mak, Elizaveta Andreiushina, Elena Dubinkina, and Ted Sanders. "Connective Use by Bilinguals and Monolinguals with SLI." *Bilingualism: Language and Cognition* 20, no. 1 (2017): 98–113.

Unsworth, Sharon, Froso Argyri, L. Cornips, Aafke Hulk, Antonella Sorace, and Ianthi Maria Tsimpli. "The Role of Age of Onset and Input in Early Child Bilingualism in Greek and Dutch." *Applied Psycholinguistics* 35, no. 4 (2014): 765–805.

Unsworth, Sharon. "Age and Input in the Acquisition of Grammatical Gender in Dutch." *Second Language Research* 24, no. 3 (2008): 365–396.

Unsworth, Sharon. "Assessing the Role of Current and CUMULATIVE Exposure in Simultaneous Bilingual Acquisition: The Case of Dutch Gender." *Bilingualism: Language and Cognition* 16, no. 1 (2013): 86–110.

# PART 5

*Transfer / Intercultural Competence Approach*

CHAPTER 15

# Different Frames of Reference [The Thing about Dutch Windows]

*Debbie Cole*

1      Introduction[1]

It is the appreciation of the relativity of the form of thought which results from linguistic study that is perhaps the most liberalizing thing about it. What fetters the mind and benumbs the spirit is ever the dogged acceptance of absolutes.

EDWARD SAPIR in *The Grammarian and His Language* (1924, 155)

Intercultural communication programs are by nature interdisciplinary, drawing as they do on expertise in a range of scholarly traditions, including communication, linguistics, anthropology, literature, media studies, history, translation, and psychology to name only a few. This chapter provides a text for use in higher education classrooms to engage students in reflexive discussions around the challenge of balancing etic and emic approaches to linguistic and cultural phenomena, a process which is "a basic fundamental characteristic that constitutes intercultural research itself" (Ten Thije 2016, 584). I have written it with intercultural communication teachers and students specifically in mind, but with the hope that it could also be useful to students and teachers in the various intra-disciplinary traditions that contribute to intercultural communication education and research. This chapter takes up the familiar observation that our well-articulated non-essentialist theories about human identity behaviors in language seem to continue to have only limited effects on public discourse, scholarly and educational practices, and institutional language policies (Denham and Lobeck 2010; Dervin 2012; Holliday and McDonald 2019). This is noticeable in the continued use of the constantly shifting concept 'diversity' and more recently, 'superdiversity,' for example, to refer to essentialized group-level differences rather than to the performance of varied personae

---

1   Written in part as a response to Langendoen (2018).

and ways of speaking within a given context – the latter perspective is now firmly established in third wave sociolinguistics (Eckert 2017) and linguistic anthropology (Agha 2007; Cole 2010; Cole 2020). It is also noticeable in the maintenance of nationalist standard practices within classroom assessment, where despite our charge to facilitate our students' multilingual repertoires and our understanding of the benefits of embracing inclusive multilingual modes and language policies (Backus et al. 2013; Hall 2013; Chatsis et al. 2013), we regularly continue to enforce variants of the ideology of strict linguistic partitioning and the ideology of the superiority of nationalist standard varieties (Meadows 2010; Cole and Meadows 2013).

Sometimes, when we are paying attention, we recognize the contradictions between our own theorizing and practicing. At other times, our insightful students point it out to us. The goal of this chapter is to provide support for making the choice not to throw up our hands in despair in those moments when we find ourselves wondering, with chagrin, how it could happen that we are seeing yet another final exam or thesis report in which the writer is seemingly no more aware of the essentialist framing in their language than they were when they started our courses, or when we catch ourselves, unawares, 'blocking' rather than 'threading' un-self-consciously (Holliday 2016).

This chapter also aims to acknowledge our scholarly and pedagogical reluctances to embrace and enact some of the practical implications of our non-essentialist theorizing, which I argue is perhaps similarly visible in the strict disciplinary partitioning and standardization of the texts we produce and invite our students to read and reproduce. Faculty members who teach in intercultural communication classrooms regularly publish within a particular, mono-disciplinary tradition, and students produce thesis projects and course assignments within our courses that typically reflect the standards and divisions between our various disciplines. It is a challenge to apply a non-essentialist mode of production or means of assessment to the language performances (presentations, exams, theses, internship reports) that we require of our students in order to demonstrate their learning. This text draws on writing styles from literature, pedagogy, formal linguistics, and anthropology in an attempt to perform one possible application of non-essentialist thinking to scholarly text production. It invites further discussion and reflection on the ways in which our well-established theorizing could have other practical impacts then it currently does.

We proceed as follows. We start with a personal reflection on ethnographic observations that formed my category of 'Dutch windows.' We will link this reflection to the concept of essentialism as it is generally used and critiqued within the social sciences. Then we will turn to Edward Sapir's ideas of equality and grading and his two part definition of language in order to synthesize practical implications for teaching and learning in interlingual, interdisciplinary, intercultural classrooms.

2      **The Thing about Dutch Windows**

    there's this thing about living in the Netherlands
    that you might've noticed
    or you might not have noticed
    or you might've noticed but noticed differently than i noticed,
    but in any case
    i will describe
    what i've noticed
    as i've noticed it
    here
    in the hopes that
    you may find
    some interesting
    similarities and differences
    between my (not) noticings and yours.

    the thing is the windows.

    more accurately,
    it's the windows
    and the window frames,
    the window frames and the things the windows frame,
    and the things that together produce the frame
    through which, for a moment
    or for a couple of moments
    you experience a vision,
    inviting you to respond with delight
    at the window framer's
    invitation
    to look in.

Let the set 'Dutch windows' be comprised of all and only windows in the Netherlands.[2]

Dutch windows vary widely in form. In fact, like all windows everywhere, each Dutch window is unique. But the category 'Dutch windows' is identifiable from other categories of windows by a number of regularly recurring tendencies sharing a range of identifiable characteristics.

If you are completely unfamiliar with Dutch windows, because you have yet to have the opportunity to visit the Netherlands or you have not previously heard about them or seen pictures of them, a brief description of what for me are the distinguishing characteristics defining the 'norm' of this particular open series may be useful.

A Dutch window is large. The glass pane seems big. It is on the bottom floor of a two or three story brick building. It takes up at least a half of the street–facing facade on the ground floor. The building was built, and is currently being used, as a family home. The window looks into a living room, or onto a dining room table, or in some cases, into a kitchen. The visible space is organized around principles of form and function which suggest attention to ease of use on the one hand and elegance on the other. I have the feeling, looking in, that I am peering into a shop that sells living rooms or gazing at an installation at a museum, so meticulously arranged is the scene. On some viewing occasions, the people who live in the space beyond the window are visible, going about their daily routines in plain sight of passersby. There are bicycles parked outside. As a viewer, I am often within two meters of the window glass. On other occasions, the blinds are closed, and the frame presents a blank opaque screen, but often with a diorama display along the lower edge, constructed of all manner of things that might include an arrangement of flowers, some books in the process of being read, a snoozing cat, some leafy mint, a few toys ....

This is a description of a 'normal Dutch window.' In the Netherlands, such window scenes are unremarkable.

I find them remarkable.

> let me pause to say,
> dank jullie wel.
> je ziet er zo mooi uit!

---

2   This set is differentiable from the set 'all windows not in the Netherlands,' and together, these two sets form the larger set 'all windows on planet earth.' Both of these sub-sets contain many other smaller potentially identifiable sets in which the distribution of windows across the planet, with or without reference to national boundaries, can be organized.

## 3 The Essentialism Problem

> Lord Vetinari has a black coach.
> Other people also have black coaches.
> Therefore, not everyone in a black coach is Lord Vetinari.
>
> It was an important philosophical insight Moist, to his regret, had forgotten in the heat of the moment.
> PRATCHETT 2007, 91

Essentialism is a concept used in the social sciences to talk about a tendency in human discourse to represent individuals as, at their essence, members of identifiable groups. In writing and speaking, we label categories of people (men, women, people with brown hair, Americans, Indonesians, Dutch speakers, people who have black coaches, etc.) as part of our description of individuals. Using these labels allows us to make inferences about a person's expected preferences and behaviors, expectations which are based on prior personal experiences with other individuals to whom that label has been applied or based on prior knowledge shared with us second hand by others. This essentialist labelling process is useful (in Dutch, *wel handig*) because it gives us a shortcut to knowing how to perform appropriate models of behavior which we hope will lead to successful interactions with others. If I know, for example, that people in the Netherlands are at ease with going about many of their daily activities in plain view of their neighbors, then I can also learn to be at ease with leaving my blinds open while I sit down to dinner with my family or by the window to read.

But there is a logical insight that gets violated when we over rely on essentialist labeling. The fact that a category label can be applied to a particular individual does not necessarily entail that that individual possesses the particular characteristic that is being focused on as a category-defining characteristic at a specific moment of talk. A person can claim a Dutch identity and yet think that the business of leaving one's window wide open to others' view is an undesirable way to behave. Having this perspective would not make this imaginary individual any less Dutch, because there are many characteristics used to define the category label 'Dutch' and because not all members of a category need possess all of the category's defining characteristics. In fact the minimal number of defining characteristics that are needed for any individual to be categorizable as 'Dutch' is one ('speaks Dutch' for example, or 'eats *stamppot*'). This does not entail, however, that possessing a particular characteristic automatically makes the characteristic–possessing entity a member of the category (one may speak Dutch but not *be* Dutch). So while essentialism clearly enables category formation, an overreliance on essentialist thinking can lead to cases of mistaken identity, like concluding that someone speaking Dutch *is* Dutch because of their language use or assuming that someone not speaking Dutch in a context where Dutch is expected is *not* Dutch. Or to link to Pratchett's literary phrasing above, though we may know that Vetinari has a black coach, if we happen to see a black coach before us, we cannot be sure we will find Vetinari inside this particular black coach.

While essentialism is an inherent property of categorization processes that can enable successful interactions based on correctly surmised assumptions, it can also lead us to faulty assumptions or to faulty expectations about individuals. An explicit awareness of this dual nature of group categorization processes has particular and important implications for intercultural communication educators and learners. Thus, a recurring learning goal of intercultural communication curricula is that students be able recognize this duality and be able to explicitly acknowledge inaccuracies that may arise when we apply category labels in speaking and writing.

## 4  How Momentary Equality Underlies Categorical Thinking

An underlying process of human habitual thought that supports category formation and use is our ability to presuppose the sufficient equality of two or more entities for the purpose of comparison with respect to some feature of 'alikeness.'[3] In 1944, Edward Sapir argued that we would be more accurate in our representation of the comparable elements of our realities if we recognized that what counts as equal is a temporary alignment of a particular shared feature of the two entities being compared. In other words, when X equals Y, it does so only for a moment. Before and after the moment of comparison, potentially comparable features are moving along multiple scales of comparison such that it is only at the moment of comparison that the whole array of potentially comparable characteristics are temporarily frozen so that a subset of the constantly fluctuating characteristics may be focused on for the purpose of comparison.

When we are making a comparison, it is like we are making a 'let statement': Let X be equal to Y. It is as if in my multiple experiences viewing different windows in the Netherlands I said to myself, 'let this window viewed at this moment be equivalently 'Dutch' to some other window viewed at a previous moment in time.'

---

3  See Ten Thije, this volume, on the concept of *Tertium Comparationis*.

In thinking about training students in non-essentialist thinking, it might be useful to ask ourselves and them the following question: What would it sound like or look like to explicitly recognize that what counts as equal in our categorization processes is only temporarily equal? In other words, to ask ourselves, what are we letting be equal in this comparison?

## 5    Languages as Complete and Distinct Systems of Reference

By definition, all of our talk about essentialist and non-essentialist thinking happens using language. The reflexive awareness around essentialism we want our students to acquire and exhibit would also be evidenced, and presumably assessed, in their use of language. If non-essentialist thinking and speaking is a learning goal for intercultural communication programs, we must be working on the assumption that students come in not being able to articulate it but will leave with the ability to do so after we've done some collaborative teaching and learning. Since language is both where the problem lies and the solution to the problem, and since reflexive awareness with respect to language use is one of our assessable goals, let us clarify what we mean by 'language' before returning to the question posed at the end of the previous paragraph.

Let us take our definition from Edward Sapir, who was read by both Noam Chomsky and by Dell Hymes (founders of two very different and schools of thought on how to define language):

1. Language is a complete system of reference
2. Language is a distinct system of reference

We can break this down, starting with what we mean by 'reference.' Referring, or talking about characteristics of our experience, is one of the things we do with language.[4] Referring is what we do when we point our finger at something that you and I can both see and then share the experience of focusing our attention on that thing. An example of how this works would be me pointing and saying to you, 'Look at that bird!' I manipulate the airflow coming up through my oral cavity to produce a soundwave moment that you recognize from prior experiences of similar soundwave moments. Your previous expe-

---

4   Referring is but one of language's functions, though it is the one that has received the most scholarly attention (Hill 2008). Jakobson listed six other known functions besides the referential: Emotive, poetic, phatic, conative, and metalingual (Jakobson 1960).

riences with sound waves of this type have regularly occurred at the same moment as your attention was directed at an animate life form (or a visual representation of an animate life form) possessing a set of shared characteristics including, but not limited, to similarities in shape and form as well as similarities of movement through space. I say 'bird' and you know what I mean because there is sufficient equality between the various examples and memories you have from prior interactions for you to be able to make a reliable connection between the signifier 'bird' and the signified creature. That is reference.

Any human language is a complete system of reference. It is a 'system,' because it is made up of parts that can be put together in predictable ways: Sounds can be combined systematically into words; words can be combined systematically into sentences. The system is complete because anything that can be referred to or said something about in one language can be referred to or said something about in any human language. Langendoen (2018) highlights Sapir's (1924) point that if a language has not been used to refer to a particular something or to say a particular something before (and is therefore without a conventionalized way of referring to that particularity), this nonexistence is a problem for the language's users to solve, not a problem inherent in the language as a system of reference itself. Langendoen uses different base systems of numbers as an example to illustrate the logical validity of this fact about language: Both a base two and a base ten number system can be used to represent the same infinite set of possible numbers, and are therefore both complete.

Any human language is also a distinct system of reference. In order for something to be distinct, there has to be something else from which that first something can be differentiated. Languages are distinct because they are systematically different from each other. And this difference, Sapir argues and his intellectual grandson, Langendoen, demonstrates to be logically true, means that speaking in one language involves the use of a frame of reference that is different from using any other language. Using different frames of reference produces different *form feelings*. Sapir explains it like this:

> To pass from one language to another is psychologically parallel to passing from one geometrical system of reference to another. The environing world which is referred to is the same for either language; the world of points is the same in either frame of reference. But the formal method of approach to the expressed item of experience, as to the given point in space, is so different that the resulting feeling of orientation can be the same neither in the two languages nor in the two frames of refer-

ence. Entirely distinct, or at least measurably distinct, formal adjustments have to be made and these differences have their psychological correlates.

SAPIR 2008, 170[5]

Notice how embedded in this two part definition of language the existence of languages, in the plural, are.

## 6 Learning and Thinking through Different Language Frames

Knowing that languages themselves enable, require, and produce multiple, distinct frames of reference has implications for dealing with the problems raised by essentialist thinking and practices. With respect to languages themselves, multilingual articulations provide us with a way to share the experience of looking through different frames. Intercultural communication programs are an ideal place for this to occur, given the way we recruit our students, offer our programs, and given the prior training and Interests students typically bring to our programs. Such double or multiple takes through at least two different language frames may work as kind of inoculation against essentialist speaking, which is one of our dogged adherences to absolutes.

Intercultural communication programs are also explicitly interdisciplinary, which makes them multilingual, or multi-repertoirial, á la Blommaert (2010), in another sense. Students in our programs are often asked to adapt from one course to the next, and sometimes within the same course, to the disciplinary practices, jargon, and narrative traditions from different scholarly perspectives. We can take linguistics, which is but one disciplinary perspective common in intercultural communication programs, as an example. There are strands of our research profiles that run from the competence, cognitivist, formal traditions and there are strands that run from the performance, interactionalist, functional traditions. Researchers working within these traditions are still figuring out how to talk to each other (Hall 2013), and one way to get us talking to each other better might be to train our students to speak in both traditions.

Perhaps we can train our students to be able to articulate the ways in which languages are both complete as well as distinct frames of reference within both the cognitive and the social traditions. Both frames of reference provide empirical data. Both frames of reference are relevant to our understanding of what

---

5  Originally published in 1924 in *American Mercury*, volume 1.

languages are and what we use them to do. Both frames of reference are necessary for a complete understanding of the relations that hold between humans as a species and their capacities for semiotic behavior, i.e. their ability to produce and make sense of signs, tokens of reference, and fragments of referentially specified information. To be accurate and complete we need to say both. This does not mean that both things need always to be said in every context, which is to say that specialization and disciplinary focus are still useful. Rather *saying both* entails that an observation of human communicative behaviors through a social frame accompanied by an observation of the same behaviors through a cognitive frame provides a more complete, more accurate, more precise, more integrated, and more elegant description and understanding of the relevant facts of those observations.

We are now ready to return to our question above: 'What would it sound like or look like to explicitly recognize that what counts as equal in our categorization processes is equal only temporarily? How can we teach with this? How can we learn this?'

## 7  Some Ideas for Practice

So one thick, red thread that runs through intercultural communication curricula is anti-essentialism. Teachers regularly provide and elicit evidence of negative consequences resulting from thinking in essentialist ways, and students regularly agree that essentialism should be avoided. Sometimes, students will ask, 'So what should I do now? Knowing that talking in essentialist ways can have some distorting effects on representing reality, what can I do in my research and daily life to be aware of it and to avoid it when I need to?' Here are some categories of ideas I am working on to be able to answer these questions for myself in my own teaching practices. Perhaps one or more of them will be useful to you too.

### 7.1  *Articulate the Principles*

When teaching and learning about languages and cultures, categorization and some level of essentializing is necessary and unavoidable (Cole and Meadows 2013). Two principles that we can articulate explicitly and consistently to assist us with being accurate and precise when we use categorical labels for sociolinguistic phenomena are 'Some, but not all; Sometimes, but not always' and 'Categorical equality is momentary and transitional.'

'Some, but not all; Sometimes, but not always' helps keep in focus the fact that generalizations are mitigated comparisons: Sometimes but not always, some, but not all, Dutch windows are large. As social scientists, we have been practicing working with this principle for a while, so examples from conversation and published texts abound. A recent review article on family talk in postindustrial, middle–class contexts includes generalizations in which I have italicized the ways that the authors have mitigated their statements using this principle: "Parental directives *often* took the form of polite requests or appeals, e.g., 'Can you take this [trash bag] out for me please?' In 22 of these families, children *frequently* ignored, resisted, or refused to help" (Ochs and Kremer Sadik 2015, 95 (emphasis added)). As teachers, we can explicitly teach students this principle by providing models of mitigated generalizations in our own speech and writing, by highlighting models in texts we read together, and by encouraging students to articulate their own mitigated statements of generalization.

The 'Categories are constantly in flux; Equality is momentary and transitional' principle keeps in focus the momentariness of categorical equality, which is to say that token A can be equated with token B for the purposes of current comparison. It incorporates into our stated observation temporal (historical) and spatial (geographic) attributes of the observation: This Dutch window is sufficiently similar to be comparable to that Dutch window at a particular moment in time from a particular point of view. Articulating this principle may prove to be a bit trickier than articulating the previous one. A reason for this is that Sapir's insight that categorical equality is momentary is, at least in my experience, explicitly articulated less often in conversation or in published texts. Perhaps this lower frequency (or perceived frequency) has something to do with the fact that this principle refers to the act of sorting experience into categories (a metacognitive behavior) rather than to particular members of the categories or to the categories themselves.

Another reason this principle may be challenging to articulate is that our scholarly, rhetorical, and attitudinal practices (as well as our daily routines more generally) rely on the reassuring notion that tokens of meaning as well as instantiations of categories of objects will be interpretable and manipulatable in the 'same' way regardless of when and where we encounter them. Once I know how to open one book and begin reading it for example, I can skillfully open and begin reading another. (That is of course until I encounter a book which requires holding in another orientation or reading in a different direction.)

This kind of accuracy is challenging for a variety of reasons, one of which is that articulating the momentariness of equality makes the evaluation of equality by the articulator explicit. This kind of accuracy incorporates an evaluation of equality between items (or observations), which are necessarily not only temporally and/or spatially separated but which are also constituted of identifying characteristics that are themselves in spatio-temporal flux. Such articulations are complex and take longer to say.

## 7.2   Try Saying Things Differently

Two practices that we can enact consistently to assist us in overcoming our tendencies towards essentialist thinking and speaking are 'Say it multiple ways, using at least two frames of reference' and 'Modify our metaphors.'

By committing to the practice of 'Saying things in multiple ways, using at least two frames of reference' we can widen the range of perspectives that come to the table around any discussion. One way to do this is to have classroom practices that encourage or require key ideas to be articulated in multiple languages. This approach has the added advantages of making audible the wider range of voices and perspectives that are present in our classrooms and of exposing more of the participants to unfamiliar *form feelings*, surely a desirable outcome for any intercultural communication course.

Consciously and subconsciously we teach using metaphors (Lakoff and Johnson 1980). Processes and policies that value standardization around languages and education practice encourage us to think and talk in ways that make categorization processes seem binary (right or wrong, good or bad, category A or category B). We can modify the way we talk using metaphors like *sliding scales* and *switching gears* rather than in terms of this category or that category. For example, someone could be more or less fluent in Dutch, depending on the context, and we might smoothly switch gears between one language and another within a single conversation to account for the different needs and abilities of the relevant speakers. When categorizing people and their behaviors, 'Try moving the slider' and 'Try shifting gears' could prove to be useful metaphors to teach and think by.

## 8   Conclusion

> the thing about Dutch windows (you see)
> is that the experience of gazing repeatedly
> through a different frame
> makes me realize that i am looking (similarly)
> at a singular snapshot
> or at an ephemeral tableau,
> at a representative token
> of the set 'dutch windows'

presented perfectly
(yet differently)
once again.

## References

Agha, Asif. *Language and Social Relations*. Cambridge: Cambridge University Press, 2007.

Backus, Ad, Durk Gorter, Karlfried Knapp, Rosita Schjerve-Rindler, Jos Swanenberg, Jan D. ten Thije, and Eva Vetter. "Inclusive Multilingualism: Concept, Modes and Implications." *European Journal for Applied Linguistics* 1, no. 2 (2013): 179–215.

Blommaert, Jan. *The Sociolinguistics of Globalization*. Cambridge: Cambridge University Press, 2010.

Chatsis, Annabelle, Mizuki Miyashita, and Deborah Cole. "A Documentary Ethnography of a Blackfoot Language Course: Patterns of *Variationism* and *Standard* in the Organization of Diversity." In *The Persistence of Language: Constructing and Confronting the Past and Present in the Voices of Jane H. Hill*, edited by Shannon Bischoff, Deborah Cole, Amy Fountain, and Mizuki Miyashita, 257–290. Amsterdam: John Benjamins, 2013.

Cole, Deborah, and Bryan Meadows. "Avoiding the Essentialist Trap in Intercultural Education: Using Critical Discourse Analysis to Read Nationalist Ideologies in the Language Classroom." In *Linguistics for Intercultural Education in Language Learning and Teaching*, edited by Fred Dervin and Anthony Liddicoat, 29–47. Amsterdam: John Benjamins, 2013.

Cole, Deborah. "Enregistering Diversity: Adequation in Indonesian Poetry Performance." *Journal of Linguistic Anthropology* 20, no. 1 (2010): 1–21.

Cole, Deborah. "The Emergent Selectivity of Semiotically Playful Utterances." In *The Discursive Organization of Contact and Boundaries*, edited by Zane Goebel, Deborah Cole, and Howard Manns, 177–194. New York: Routledge, 2020.

Denham, Kristin, and Anne Lobeck. *Linguistics at School: Language Awareness in Primary and Secondary Education*. Cambridge: Cambridge University Press, 2010.

Dervin, Fred. "Cultural Identity, Representation and Othering." In *The Routledge Handbook of Language and Intercultural Communication*, edited by Jane Jackson, 181–194. London: Routledge, 2012.

Eckert, Penelope. "Comment: The Most Perfect of Signs. Iconicity in Variation." *Linguistics* 55, no. 5 (2017): 1197–1207.

Hall, Christopher. "Cognitive Contributions to Plurilithic Views of English and Other Languages." *Applied Linguistics* 34, no. 2 (2013): 211–223.

Hill, Jane. *The Everyday Language of White Racism*. Chichester: Wiley-Blackwell, 2008.

Holliday, Adrian, and Malcolm McDonald. "Researching the Intercultural: Intersubjectivity and the Problem with Postpositivism." *Applied Linguistics* 41, no. 5 (2019): 1–20.

Holliday, Adrian. "Difference and Awareness in Cultural Travel: Negotiating Blocks and Threads." *Language and Intercultural Communication* 16, no. 3 (2016): 318–331.

Jakobson, Roman. "Closing statement: Linguistics and Poetics." In *Style in Language*, edited by Thomas Sebeok, 339–349. Cambridge, Massachusetts: The M.I.T. Press, 1960.

Lakoff, George, and Mark Johnson. *Metaphors we Live by*. Chicago: University of Chicago Press, 1980.

Langendoen, Terence. "Languages as Complete and Distinct Systems of Reference." In *Essays on Linguistic Realism*, edited by Christina Behme and Martin Neef, 255–270. Amsterdam: John Benjamins, 2018.

Meadows, Bryan. "'Like My Tutor and Stuff, People I Would Talk to': Laying Claim to Imagined National Communities of Practice in Language Learner Discourse." *Critical Inquiry in Language Studies* 7, no. 2–3 (2010): 88–111.

Ochs, Elinor, and Tamar Kremer-Sadlik. "How Postindustrial Families Talk." *Annual Review of Anthropology* 44 (2015): 87–103.

Pratchett, Terry. *Making Money*. New York: Harper Collins, 2007.

Sapir, Edward. "Grading, A Study in Semantics." *Philosophy of Science* 11, no. 2 (1944): 93–116.

Sapir, Edward. "The Grammarian and His Language." In *The Collected Works of Edward Sapir, I: General Linguistics*, edited by Pierre Swiggers, 167–176. Berlin: Mouton de Gruyter, 2008.

Thije, Jan D. ten. "Intercultural Communication." In *Sprache—Kultur—Kommunikation / Language—Culture—Communication. Ein internationales Handbuch zu Linguistik als Kulturwissenschaft. An International Handbook of Linguistics as Cultural Study*, edited by Ludwig Jäger, Werner Holly, Peter Krapp, Samuel Weber and Simone Heekeren, 581–594. Berlin: Mouton de Gruyter, 2016.

CHAPTER 16

# Education, Mobility and Higher Education: Fostering Mutual Knowledge through Peer Feedback

*Emmanuelle Le Pichon-Vorstman and Michèle Ammouche-Kremers*

1       Introduction: A Response to Student Mobility and Diversity

In the last thirty years, cross-border student mobility has been encouraged worldwide resulting in an increasing internationalization of higher education. Studying abroad is invariably considered as a beneficial experience, not to say a marker of success, as it offers a more rounded global education experience. In Europe, the Erasmus Programme[1] was established in 1987 to promote such mobility and nearly 10 million students have studied abroad since its creation.[2] Often considered as one of the best Gateways to Europe, the Netherlands has become an attractive study destination for international students and, although not an anglophone country, English is widely spoken and fast becoming the lingua franca in most Dutch universities. The peer-feedback experiment presented in this chapter was developed at Utrecht University, where nearly ten percent of students are internationals, whose share is growing steadily with both short-term Erasmus exchange students and long-term diploma seeking ones. Education abroad often means experiencing foreign cultures, practicing new languages and developing new skills to deal with increasingly complex intercultural situations. Yet, as students' international mobility is intensifying, it is surprising that opportunities for interactions between local and non-local students remain scarce. Additionally, adaptation of local academic programs to the changing student population has proven challenging and has failed to meet students' linguistic and cultural diversity. It could therefore be argued that the higher education system has failed to provide students and staff with the linguistic, cultural and methodological support necessary to foster intercultural communication opportunities generated by international student mobility in general and exchange programs in particular (Herzog-Punzenberger, Le Pichon-Vorstman and Siarova 2017).

---

1   European Community Action Scheme for the Mobility of University Students.
2   https://ec.europa.eu/commission/presscorner/detail/en/MEMO_17_83.

One original approach to support interaction between local and international students is the implementation of the 'peer-feedback project' that started at Utrecht University, a practice where language students, hereafter referred to as language learners, receive feedback by international students, called language assistants. In exchange, these language assistants can receive training in Dutch (the local language) to facilitate integration in local social and academic life, or in another language in the case of an international peer. When we started the program, we used the expression 'native speaker' for commodity, allowing for the reservations expressed by Kramsch (1997). However, very early on, we became aware of the loss of pertinence of this term from a societal and scholarly standpoint (see also Holliday 2015; Lowe et al. 2016) and decided to abandon it. The language assistants recruited into the project were students who identified as highly proficient in the language they chose to review as peers. Although the benefits of peer feedback have been widely documented (see for instance, Jahin 2012), the interest for its specific benefits in higher education is quite recent and a review of the literature demonstrates the uniqueness of the multilingual intercultural out-of-class peer feedback in place at Utrecht University.

## 2  Rationale

### 2.1  *Genesis and Development*

In 2012, the peer-feedback project was started as an experiment in the French department of Utrecht University. Today, the program spans three faculties and seven languages. Originally, students who identified as highly proficient in French, both Erasmus exchange students and international students enrolled in degree programs, provided their French language learner peers with feedback on their academic writing tasks at the Bachelor level. The feedback sessions were both oral and written. The initiative stemmed from both students and teachers' wishes. Students regretted the limited practice of oral French during class due to time pressure as well as the absence of contact with French speakers outside of class. Students were also interested in receiving more individual feedback. Additionally, if a minimum level of French is required to enroll in the French Bachelor program, no maximum level is mentioned. As a result, some students can be bilingual whilst others are at lower levels of language learning. This resulted in frustration on the part of the most proficient students who felt they were wasting their time as their language skills were not utilized to the fullest. On the side of the teachers, there was frustration at the amount of correction time spent on form at the expense of content.

In 2013–2014, when we evaluated the project, it emerged that nine language assistants conducted 191 feedback sessions, to a total of 573 hours of involvement in the feedback process (Le Pichon-Vorstman and Van Beuningen 2014). The evaluations showed that the peer-feedback project ministered to the above-mentioned needs and benefited three target groups. As expected, language learners, the first group, perceived an improvement in their writing skills in the target language. They reported a greater knowledge of, control over, and awareness of form-related aspects of their writing in the target language (e.g., grammar, spelling, punctuation). They were satisfied with the twofold increase in their exposure to the language and with the opportunity to express themselves freely in the language. Their satisfaction with both the language assistants and the feedback process was high. They reported having become more self-regulated writers, and gaining metacognitive skills, confidence, and motivation (Le Pichon-Vorstman and Van Beuningen 2014). At the same time, teachers, the second group, reported being satisfied with the decrease in their workload in terms of language correction. As for the third group, language assistants, they seemed to benefit at least as much from this experience: they appreciated the opportunity to meet local students, to develop their teaching and coaching skills, and to reflect on their own language (see also Lundstrom and Baker 2009). Following these positive results, the approach was extended to the English, German, Italian and Spanish departments of Utrecht University and to University College Utrecht[3] in 2016–2017. The project was then further extended to include Dutch as well as Chinese in the following academic years. Before the COVID-19 pandemic, the number of language assistants was steadily increasing to around 50 language assistants per semester across seven languages.

## 2.2 *Originality*

Studies show that the use of peer interaction is beneficial, even "cardinal to the improvement of students' learning, because it allows students to construct knowledge through social sharing and interaction" (Bijami et al. 2013, 93) and some researchers avow that it plays a pivotal role in improving students' writing skills and learning achievements (Topping et al. 2000; Plutsky and Wilson 2004). The "social, cognitive, affective, and methodological benefits" of peer feedback are also well documented (Jahin 2012, 65). However, while peer feedback has been extensively used and studied in classrooms in primary

---

3 University College Utrecht provides English-language liberal Arts and Sciences undergraduate education.

and secondary classrooms, as it is now gaining popularity at university level, its various benefits there have also been reviewed (Chardonneau 2016) and its use documented (Landry, Jacobs and Newton 2015; Manoilov and Tardieu 2015). Notably, it has been highlighted as an important alternative to teacher feedback (Landry, Jacobs and Newton 2015). To our knowledge, however, the effect of peer feedback from an intercultural perspective has not been reported yet.

## 3    The Participants: Language Learners and Language Assistants

Apart from it taking place at the Bachelor and Master levels, this peer-feedback program is unusual because the peers, although of equal student status, are not equal status learners: the language assistants bring additional knowledge into the equation within a more flexible framework since they are, chiefly, neither from the same class, the same discipline nor the same level of competence. The students who enroll might study law, social sciences or humanities, and often find themselves at different stages in their studies. A degree-seeking French student at Bachelor level can help revise the Master's thesis of a student in the French track of Intercultural Studies while a third-year student from Great-Britain on exchange can assist first year law students with the writing of their papers in English. Interestingly, the demand for peer feedback in English has been increasing as English as a Medium of Instruction is gaining further ground outside the Humanities departments. Hence, although language learners and language assistants remain peers, they are interacting in a cross-disciplinary, plurilingual space outside the classroom, and at varying academic levels.

## 4    A Decompartmentalization to Promote Flexibility and Reciprocity

### 4.1    *Flexibility*
While retaining their symmetric status as students, language learners and language assistants have different linguistic and national backgrounds. This situation is particularly favorable for the staging of intercultural encounters: the dormant ethnocentrism of each student is confronted with the discovery of the other, whatever his or her role in the peer feedback. During their meetings, they confront their respective funds of knowledge (Moll et al. 1992). These funds of knowledge are not only languages but also norms and habits, including academic norms of their own disciplines. In doing so, culture is caught in the act, more likely stripped of the essentialist, idealized, or distorted vision linked to

nationalistic paradigms. In a way, the peer-feedback program embodies the linguistic and cultural diversity which language courses find hard to introduce.

The increasing heterogeneity and polychromatic nature of the student body is reflected in peers who often find it difficult to define themselves within the traditional categories of linguistic, cultural or even national belonging. For instance, a Spanish national has been offering feedback in French, a German student has been giving feedback in three languages, and another binational residing in yet another country most of her life felt more assured giving feedback in a language that did not formally correspond to the nationality stated in her passport. Hence, they all experienced the relativity of labelling and categorizing. In their dialogue with each other, the students witnessed the elusiveness of national and ethnic markers, tasted identity as 'fluid' and negotiated through interactions with others (see also Bucholtz and Hall 2005). In some cases, friendships developed bringing a deeper understanding and openness; in others the relationship focused exclusively on improving writing and speaking skills. Yet, even in the latter case, students thought being faced with and learning to negotiate diversity a valuable experience.

## 4.2 *Reciprocity*

In order to further promote reciprocity, the language assistants who provide feedback in the language they are proficient in can, in return, ask the students they are helping to assist them in another language. As the majority of students receiving feedback were Dutch, the language assistants could ask for help in learning some basic Dutch and finding their way around campus, Utrecht and the Netherlands, thus facilitating their academic and social integration. Sometimes language assistants can receive help in yet another language; for example, a French language assistant who is also proficient in Spanish, when helping a Spanish student of French can request Spanish conversation practice to brush up her fluency. This reciprocity principle might imply an interesting inversion of power, by reversing the roles of experts and novices. As a result, the program moves radically away from the principles of peer feedback defined as "shared incompetence" (Gass 2017). Interestingly, the latter definition was implicitly based on the monoglot ideology (Blommaert 2009) of students with homogenous competencies gathered in the same program. The diversity described as the initial motivation for the development of this program shows that this pseudo-homogeneity no longer corresponds to the changing population in higher education.

## 5 The Language Legitimacy

A crucial particularity of the program resides in the fact that language assistants have an expertise which their peers do not have thanks to their proficiency in at least one particular language. This expertise may vary and the language assistants' transmission of linguistic and cultural awareness may be hindered by a lack of didactic skills. However, they are, by definition, more competent than the students they are helping. Although not always formally trained, this (relative) expertise grants them credibility when they interact with students, comment on and critique their written and oral work. Whereas peer feedback is sometimes viewed with skepticism because the teacher is perceived as the sole authority, the language assistant's language competence is not questioned. When asked to rate their language assistants on a 1 to 5 point scale, nearly 95 percent of the students gave their language assistants a 4 or a 5. This demonstrates the students' appreciation of and confidence in their language assistants' work.

## 6 The Framework: Goals and Required Conditions for Participation

The main and initial objective of the project was to improve students' proficiency in the target language. Initially limited to written feedback, the program has been broadened in response to students' wishes. It now has three goals which can be achieved separately or together and includes written and oral feedback. Therefore, tasks of the language assistants have been specified as follows:

1. to provide feedback on written texts including Bachelor's and Master's theses;
2. to provide feedback on oral tasks, practicing oral presentations, training for oral exams;
3. to fulfill any language needs students may have.

With these objectives in mind, one of the conditions for the success of this project is the training of the language assistants to teach them the basics of a satisfactory feedback process.

### 6.1 *Training of Language Assistants*

While developing the project, and at the request of both teachers and language assistants, we decided to set up a light training for the language assistants. This initiative corroborates the recommendations of many researchers who have worked on the subject (see for instance van den Berg et al. 2006; Topping 1998). The training consists of two workshops per semester plus individual meetings at the end of the semester with the language assistants who wish to receive credits or a letter of recommendation. The setting up of this training has allowed us to overcome limitations of feedback by providing the language assistants with both the basic rules of academic conduct as well as some essentials of the theories surrounding so-called foreign or second language acquisition. Between 2016 and 2018, the evaluations show that 70 to 95 percent of the language assistants think they have received enough instructions to accomplish their tasks. All of them stated they had greatly benefited from the workshops.

### 6.1.1 Workshop 1

The first workshop starts by explaining and discussing practical information related to the language assistants' tasks[4] before moving on to how to give formative feedback on both written and oral tasks. Using past examples for clarity, the training session focuses on the language assistant's role, which is to signal potential language issues trying to avoid correction or explicit reformulation. The language learners receive their annotated work and endeavor to improve and self-correct their text. As research has shown, self-correction demands a stronger level of commitment from the student, which may lead to improved learning outcomes (Lyster and Mori 2006). After a first round of written feedback, the language assistant and language learner meet (online or in person) to discuss further improvements or remaining difficulties. One of the advantages of this two-step process is that both written and oral communication skills are practiced.

During our workshops, language assistants are encouraged to keep positive and constructive attitudes. They are also informed of the diversity of students they will communicate with as well as the various types of texts, from basic informative descriptive texts to complex argumentative theses. They are reminded that their feedback centers on textual issues. Additionally, one aim of the workshop is to raise awareness among the language assistants: although proficient speakers in their language, they may not know or be aware of the formal rules. Alternatively, the language they use may correspond to a certain variety which is not necessarily the variety taught in the language departments of the university. Reassurance is given and regardless of their formal knowledge, they are advised to work together with the student on issues they are not able to resolve by checking additional resources such as dictionaries, grammar

---

4  All practical information can be found on the Language Assistants website of Utrecht University: expectations, organization of the peer-feedback sessions, conditions to gain credits or receive a letter of recommendation, potential benefits.

books, and information online. Feedback on oral presentations focuses similarly on the linguistic dimension. Apart from pointing out morphosyntactic or spelling errors in their PowerPoints and helping the learner self-correct, assistants can also help with pronunciation in a relaxed environment, and enrich the student's text by proposing synonyms or alternative phrasing.

### 6.1.2    Workshop 2

During the follow-up workshop which takes place mid-semester, language assistants are split in groups corresponding to their language and are offered past examples to analyze and comment on. The plenary session that ensues discusses their findings as well as the experience and the challenges they have encountered as language peers, e.g., feedback techniques, recurrent mistakes and language-specific difficulties, direct versus indirect feedback, complex text revisions or any other topic of their choice. Importantly, in both workshops, particular attention is drawn to the multifaceted profile of the students requiring feedback, both linguistically and culturally. Concrete examples are given to raise awareness of cultural and individual variations, as well as the power of the one-on-one meeting to discuss possible negotiation of these situations. In addition to these two workshops, an individual meeting is conducted with the language assistants who will receive credit and/or a letter of recommendation for their work. This offers a precious opportunity to discuss their experience in more depth and to evaluate the training as well as the peer-feedback procedures.

## 7    Peer-Feedback Procedure

The peer feedback is delivered on a voluntary basis but only feedback on written texts and on oral tasks (tasks 1 & 2), which are directly linked to academic work within a course can generate credits for the language assistants;[5] importantly, credits can be granted if the required conditions have been fulfilled: a logbook must be presented listing the learners who have been helped and the number of hours spent on written and oral feedback, and a reflection report must be written respecting a set of guidelines.

At the request of the language assistant, the program manager can also provide a letter of recommendation. Those who have not been able to give enough

---

5  European Credit Transfer System, credits received at one higher education institution count towards a qualification studied for at another (ec.europa.eu).

feedback to receive credit, either by choice or because too few students asked for their help, can also receive a letter of recommendation after the fulfillment of a similar, be it lighter, set of requirements. In both cases, attendance of the training workshops is a prerequisite.

## 8  Program Manager's Role

Although language assistants work independently, the manager of the program stays informed of activities[6] and is available for any questions they may have via a non-personal email address. The manager also recruits international students in liaison with the International Offices and gives a presentation during their orientation days at the start of each semester. International degree students are invited to join by collective emails sent via the program platform. After the recruitment period, the manager is responsible for the organization of the training workshops and remains available for helping both language assistants and language learners facing difficulties.

Whereas most questions relate to practical issues, e.g., appropriate place of meetings, freedom to deviate from initial feedback, advice on how to deal with particular situations, a recurrent question concerns Master's students who must write their theses in English. For this language assistants with academic writing experience are required, and it is the task of the manager to find the most appropriate match, for example more experienced English speakers who are studying for Master's degrees themselves or, as is often the case, older language assistants who obtained a Master's or PhD at a previous university and are enrolled for a Master's degree in another field at Utrecht University.

## 9  Evaluation of the Program

Both for administrative reasons, like calculating the number of hours invested by each participant and by academic staff, and to ensure the quality of the program and its improvement, online questionnaires are sent at the end of each semester to students who have participated. For the learners, questions range from practical matters—number and duration of feedback sessions, name of the course for which the work submitted for feedback was done, means of

---

6  The manager is put in cc. in the first couple of mail exchanges at the beginning of a peer-feedback process between language assistant and language learners.

communication, language used during feedback sessions—to more substantive multiple-choice questions such as ordering the benefits of the feedback they received, grading their feedback experience or ranking the components of peer feedback they value most compared with teacher feedback. For the language assistants, questions also range from informative ones—for instance, number of students helped, number of feedback sessions per student, difficulties in communication—to prioritizing criteria in order to assess the success of a peer-feedback session. Language assistants are also asked whether the instructions they received prepared them for their tasks, whether they reached their personal targets, whether their experience has contributed to their social life in the Netherlands, and which were their main reasons for participating in the program.

## 10 The Experience of Language Learners, Language Assistants and the Teaching Community

Between 2016 and 2019, the great majority of the 127 language learners who completed the evaluation found working with a language assistant a "valuable" to "very valuable" experience. Of the 47 language assistants who responded in 2017 and 2018, around 70 percent found that giving feedback contributed to their social life in the Netherlands and more than 90 percent indicated they had reached their personal goals. While mirroring the results of the evaluations, the assistants' reflection reports provide deeper insight into the peer-feedback experience by highlighting some of the most important benefits for the three parties involved: the language learners, the language assistants, and, indirectly, the teaching community.

### 10.1 *The Language Learners*
Thanks to the one-on-one feedback from language assistants, language learners benefit from a significantly greater exposure to the language they are studying, both orally and in writing, as well as from the opportunity to converse in the target language: between 2017 and 2019, according to the language assistants, roughly 50 percent of the meetings were held solely in the target language and 30 percent were held half in English and half in the target language. Learners record better grades for their courses and a perceived improvement in their written and oral skills. Roughly 60 percent of the 127 learners who completed the online survey between 2016 and 2019 think that both their grammar and spelling and/or their understanding of text problems have improved. They also report becoming more self-regulatory writers (autonomy), an important

metacognitive skill, as well as an increased sense of competence. Such a felt increase in competence and autonomy stems from the collaborative character of the peer-feedback activity; free of power relations or assessment anxiety, the peer feedback turns into a positive experience of interdependence and trust between the peers. The students mention that they feel comfortable during the sessions, do not feel pressure or apprehension, and dare to ask questions they would not have asked in class. They also tend to be very lenient with their peers, as this quote suggests: "He did what he could to help me" (Le Pichon-Vorstman and van Beuningen 2014). The peer feedback has also proven particularly popular with language learners in the process of writing their Bachelor or Master's theses in a target language they have often not been exposed to for months due to constraints in their curriculum.

## 10.2 *The Language Assistants*

The language assistants in their reflection reports highlight several benefits which demonstrate that the giver gains at least as much as the receiver during the peer-feedback process. This corroborates Lundstrom and Baker's findings aptly entitled "To Give Is Better than to Receive: The Benefits of Peer Review to the Reviewer's Own Writing" (2009). Some of our results were expected whilst others were slightly unforeseen. As anticipated, the language assistants' participation seems to support their academic and social integration as well as to broaden their intercultural outlook. They were impressed by the plurilingual and multicultural profiles of some of the learners. The experience enriched their curriculum and the ones who envisaged a career in teaching were grateful for the opportunity to test and develop their didactic skills. Even when not contemplating a teaching career, language assistants valued the fact that their feedback activities provided them with work experience comparable to an internship. The following observations are recurrent in the reflection reports.

### 10.2.1    Perception of Personal Enrichment

"Enriching" is the term most frequently used by assistants to describe their participation in the peer-feedback program: enriching on a personal, social, cultural, academic, and didactic level. Referring to their personal development, language assistants often remark that their involvement was, "a great enrichment to my stay in Utrecht" (ES 2018),[7] "it enriched my stay in Utrecht" (EH 2018), "a real added value to my stay in Utrecht" (AP 2017), "a very interesting experience" (EN 2017), "without any doubt a positive and enriching experience

---

7   For privacy reasons, initials and date refer to the author and date of the reflection report.

for me" (UK 2014), "an enriching experience" (EC 2019). According to some, the peer-feedback program also helped them to further develop social and communication skills: "the program has improved my social and communicative skills" (MA 2019) or "it gave me the feeling of doing something useful while also improving my own social skills" (KK 2019).

10.2.2    Reported Increase in Self-Confidence and Sense of Legitimacy

Many language assistants found their voluntary work particularly rewarding, which, in turn, increased their self-confidence: "I gained more confidence and realized that my communicative skills with non-German speakers improved" (EH 2018), "I have also gained self-confidence and am more at ease when meeting people" (MR 2017). Interestingly, and less anticipated, is the fact that, in certain cases, the peer-feedback activities increased the language assistants' confidence in their own language granting them a legitimacy they sometimes questioned, as in the case of a trilingual German student using her three languages on a daily basis and grateful to be trusted in giving feedback in the three languages which define her identity. Another salient case was that of a Canadian student who was very intimidated by the fact that his French was not representative of the "Parisian French" accent. At first, he was hesitant to even join the program feeling his Quebec French accent disqualified him from becoming a language assistant. After being encouraged by the manager, he became involved in the project and reflected: "This program helped me reaffirm my confidence in my French language from an academic as well as a personal point of view" (BG 2017). Another student wrote that she had been very hurt when a French university refused her entry in its training program to become a teacher of French as a foreign language because of her Spanish nationality even though she was born in France. She stressed that the program allowed her to regain the legitimacy she had lost (M 2015).

10.2.3    Intercultural Dialogues and Mutual Enrichment

Working with both Dutch and international learners, language assistants were also enthusiastic about the intercultural benefits: "the opportunity to engage in intercultural dialogue with the students I tutored" (AM 2018), "hugely appreciated the opportunity to share my culture with foreigners who had a certain interest for France and the French language" (DM 2018), "the exchanges with students were particularly interesting as several had lived in different countries and spoke several languages. This enabled me to learn more about The Netherlands and their teaching method, but also about other countries and cultures" (OBG 2019). Interestingly, learning about culture is seen as a two-way exchange that is not limited to a target culture but serves as a means for opening up to new horizons. Some of the language assistants' remarks reflect the problematic situation of international students. They expect a stay abroad will allow them to meet the local population and to integrate into the target society. However, the situation of international students living among themselves during their exchanges has often been described. A number of the language assistants described how the program had helped them avoid international students' tendency to withdraw into themselves; in doing so, they felt that they had developed a stronger sense of belonging: "It enabled me to get an insight into the Dutch culture, something I would not have had the opportunity to if had I not signed up for this" (EN 2017).

### 10.2.4  Metalinguistic and Metacultural Awareness

Most language assistants were surprised by the time they needed to invest in their peer-feedback tasks. They also found it more challenging than they thought it would be (ES 2018). Additionally, explaining the workings of their language and culture made them realize how unaware they were of certain aspects of their language and country of belonging: "pushed me to ask questions on my own language" (EC 2019), "it was useful for my own mastery of French since I had to spend time looking up rules I myself had forgotten" (EN 2017), "I have come to know my native language from the perspective of an outsider" (LM 2020), "to conclude, this project helped me discover my own language" (DM 2018), "I never learned as much about French and France than during this time I was abroad" (CH 2019). It is interesting that language assistants mention this metalinguistic and metacultural dimension as an unexpected enrichment.

### 10.2.5  Professional Teaching Experience

Some participants started to envisage a profession they had never considered before: "the program revealed to me that I liked to explain and to teach" (BS 2019). The ones who already envisaged a career in teaching were grateful for the opportunity to test and develop their didactic skills. Others felt encouraged to get out of their comfort zone: "I think that meeting so many students from all over the world has led to the confidence I needed to make the choice to go study abroad myself" (MQ 2019). Thanks to the interdisciplinary nature of the program, another language assistant discovered the field of intercultural studies via the work of her students and considered enrolling in a Master's program in the subject. All in all, these testimonials demonstrate that the peer-feedback experience enriched the language assistants' lives as well as their curricula. They felt both humbled and emboldened by the tokens of gratitude from the students they had helped and valued the confidence they invested in them. Some had participated in tandem initiatives in their home university but were so convinced by the multilayered approach of our peer feedback that they wanted to introduce a similar project upon their return.

## 10.3  The Teachers

Teachers approach the peer-feedback program in various ways, although the great majority view it positively. One teacher who openly refused to participate had a purist vision of languages and language learning: she expressed her fear of subjecting her students to language assistants without professional legitimacy and therefore likely to "make mistakes." Another teacher using language assistants for the first time in her class was concerned about the above average quality of some of her students' work and called the manager questioning the integrity of the assistants in their assistance. The joint examination of the various versions of the work in question made her realize how much had been done by her students, both concerning the language and the organization of the argument, under the guidance of the language assistant. From then on, this teacher systematically involved peer feedback in her classes. In fact, some teachers choose to include language assistants in their classes on a regular basis throughout the year.

As expected, the main advantage reported by all the teachers involved was the correction time that the language assistants saved them, enabling them to focus on academic content, a benefit which is often mentioned in earlier studies (e.g., Burns and Foo 2012; Higgins, Hartley and Skelton 2002). Notably supervisors of Bachelor and Master's theses appreciate being able to focus on content-driven guidance instead of spending time addressing language issues. This is a very interesting result in the light of the increasing mobility of students in higher education who often have to write in English or the language of the discipline but not necessarily the one the student is most proficient in. This difficulty requires adaptations on the part of the academic body comparable to the one we are proposing.

## 11  Conclusion

The originality of the program we have presented lies in its taking advantage of international students' abilities which are not usually taken into account during a stay abroad: their foreign language skills. Set up as a support program on a voluntary basis, the program capitalizes on students' skills that would otherwise probably remain hidden or marginalized in the context of their stay abroad. By highlighting these skills, the program allows the students acting as language assistants to rediscover parts of themselves while discovering the other in a personal encounter. While the focus of the program is officially on language, issues of culture such as norms, habits, or ways of living and studying appear naturally in the students' discourse regardless of their tasks in the project and often empower them to open up to new horizons. They discover that assigning a language and culture to another is often arbitrary and much more complex than stereotypical imagery may suggest. We do not pretend that this program offers a solution to all the questions raised by student mobility. However, these results show that the participation in intercultural interactions framed and formalized by the program can significantly increase chances of intercultural growth. This has already been proposed by others as a possible consequence of stays abroad, be it infrequent and certainly not systematic (see for instance Sobkowiak 2019). It is clear that the approach of the peer-feedback project, taking advantage of students' language skills which would otherwise be ignored, allows them to add an important intercultural dimension to their stay abroad. This dimension involves the discovery of the other, which is inseparable from the rediscovery of oneself. From a theoretical point of view, it is interesting that this program has forced us to renounce the term 'native speaker' and to denounce with the students what others have called 'native speakerism' (Holliday 2006; 2015; Holliday, Aboshiha and Swan 2015). The indulgence shown by the language learners towards their peers is remarkable in the sense that it justifies the term 'peers' in the project despite the differences mentioned in the introduction of this paper (differences in language proficiency, domain of expertise or academic discipline). The trust placed by the learners in the assistants legitimizes them not only in the language in question but also in their belonging to a given linguistic and cultural community, allowing them to reevaluate their own identity. Several of the above examples, which others might have called "rich points" (Agar 1994), have shown how individual encounters between local and international students in a university setting, with minimal supervision but with academic recognition, has brought about a range of intercultural benefits.

## 11.1 *Challenges and Further Development*

Since the start of the 2019/20 academic year, the program has been brought under the umbrella of a larger program, called 'Academic Buddy program.' The ambition of this new program is to stimulate and support even more meaningful interaction between local and international students. Given its success, the goals and mode of functioning of the peer-feedback program remained unchanged. However, the ambition is to introduce it university wide as well as to offer peer feedback to students at graduate and post-graduate levels. Such a scaling up is challenging in terms of logistics and adaptation. It also offers new opportunities to bridge disciplines, to reach a larger part of the student population in need of improving its oral and written language proficiency, and to foster intercultural encounters. In doing so, we are confident that it will raise awareness of the crucial role languages play in education in redefining identity and will continue to offer insights into how higher education can reinvent itself to better serve its multilingual and multicultural populations.

**References**

Agar, Michael. *Language Shock. Understanding the Culture of Conversation*. New York: William Morrow & Co. Inc, 1994.

Berg, Ineke van den, Wilfried Admiraal, and Albert Pilot. "Design Principles and Outcomes of Peer Assessment in Higher Education." *Studies in Higher Education* 31, no. 3 (2006): 341–356. https://doi.org/10.1080/03075070600680836.

Bijami, Maryam, Seyyed Hosein Kashef, and Maryam Sharafi Nejad. Peer Feedback in Learning English Writing: Advantages and Disadvantages." *Journal of Studies in Education* 3, no. 4 (2013): 91–97.

Blommaert, Jan. "Language, Asylum, and the National Order." *Current Anthropology* 50, no. 4 (2009): 415–441. https://doi.org/10.1086/600131.

Bucholtz, Mary, and Kira Hall. "Identity and Interaction: A Sociocultural Linguistic Approach." *Discourse Studies* 7, no. 4–5 (2005): 585–614. https://doi.org/10.1177/1461445605054407.

Burns, Caroline, and Martin Foo. "How Is Feedback Used?—The International Student Response to a Formative Feedback Intervention." *The International Journal of Management Education* 11, no. 3 (2013): 174–183. https://doi.org/10.1016/j.ijme.2013.06.001.

Chardonneau, Lucie. "L'évaluation et la rétroaction par les pairs en enseignement supérieur." *Bulletin de Veille* no. 6 (2016): 1–5. https://www.innovation-pedagogique.fr/article569.html.

Gass, Susan M. *Input, Interaction, and the Second Language Learner*. New York: Routledge, 2017. https://doi.org/10.4324/9781315173252.

Herzog-Punzenberger, Barbara, Emmanuelle Le Pichon-Vorstman, and Hanna Siarova. *Multilingual Education in the Light of Diversity: Lessons Learned*. Luxembourg: Publications Office of the European Union, 2017. https://doi.org/10.2766/71255.

Higgins, Richard, Peter Hartley, and Alan Skelton. "The Conscientious Consumer: Reconsidering the Role of Assessment Feedback in Student Learning." *Studies in Higher Education* 27, no. 1 (2002): 53–64. https://doi.org/10.1080/03075070120099368.

Holliday, Adrian. "Native-Speakerism." *ELT Journal* 60, no. 4 (2016): 385–387. https://doi.org/10.1093/elt/ccl030.

Holliday, Adrian. "Native-speakerism: Taking the Concept Forward and Achieving Cultural Belief." In *(En)Countering Native-speakerism*, edited by Anne Swan, Pamela Aboshiha and Adrian Holliday, 11–25. New York: Palgrave Macmillan, 2015.

Jahin, Jamal Hamed. "The Effect of Peer Reviewing on Writing Apprehension and Essay Writing Ability of Prospective EFL Teachers." *Australian Journal of Teacher Education* 37, no. 11 (2012): 60–84 http://dx.doi.org/10.14221/ajte.2012v37n11.3.

Kramsch, Claire. "Guest Column: The Privilege of the Nonnative Speaker." *PMLA* 112, no. 3 (1997): 359–369. Accessed February 28, 2021: http://www.jstor.org/stable/462945.

Landry, Ashley, Shoshanah Jacobs, and Genevieve Newton. "Effective Use of Peer Assessment in a Graduate Level Writing Assignment: a Case Study." *International Journal of Higher Education* 4, no. 1 (2015): 38–51. https://doi.org/10.5430/ijhe.v4n1p38.

Le Pichon-Vorstman, Emmanuelle, and Catherine van Beuningen. 2014. "Identifying Success Factors of Expert-peer Feedback in L2 Academic Writing." Unpublished paper. Conference on Writing Research, Amsterdam.

Lowe, Robert J., and Marek Kiczkowiak. "Native-speakerism and the Complexity of Personal Experience: A Duoethnographic Study." *Cogent Education* 3, no. 1 (2016). https://doi.org/10.1080/2331186X.2016.1264171.

Lundstrom, Kristi, and Wendy Baker. "To Give Is Better than to Receive: The Benefits of Peer Review to the Reviewer's Own Writing." *Journal of Second Language Writing* 18, no. 1 (2009): 30–43. https://doi.org/10.1016/j.jslw.2008.06.002.

Lyster, Roy, and Hirohide Mori. "Interactional Feedback and Instructional Counterbalance." *Studies in Second Language Acquisition* 28, no. 2 (2006): 269–300. Accessed March 4, 2021, http://www.jstor.org/stable/44487069.

Manoilov, Pascale, and Claire Tardieu. "Rétroaction corrective et reprise dans le contexte de l'apprentissage en tandems Français-Anglais à l'université." *Cahiers de l'ACEDLE* 12, no. 3 (2015). https://doi.org/10.4000/rdlc.986.

Moll, Luis, Cathy Amanti, Deborah Neff, and Norma Gonzalez. "Funds of Knowledge for Teaching: Using a Qualitative Approach to Connect Homes and Classrooms." *Theory into Practice* 31, no. 2 (1992): 132–141. https://doi.org/10.1080/00405849209543534.

Plutsky, Susan, and Barbara A. Wilson. "Comparison of Three Methods for Teaching and Evaluating Writing: A Quasi-Experimental Study." *Delta Pi Epsilon Journal* 46, no. 1 (2004): 50–61.

Rollinson, Paul. "Using Peer Feedback in the ESL Writing Class." *ELT Journal* 59, no. 1 (2005): 23–30. https://doi.org/10.1093/elt/cci003.

Sobkowiak, Paweł. "The Impact of Studying Abroad on Students' Intercultural Competence: An Interview Study." *Studies in Second Language Learning and Teaching* 9, no. 4 (2019): 681–710. https://doi.org/10.14746/ssllt.2019.9.4.6.

Swan, Anne, Pamela Aboshiha, and Adrian Holliday. *(En)countering Native-Speakerism: Global Perspectives*. New York: Palgrave Macmillan, 2015.

Topping, Keith, Jillian Nixon, Jennifer Sutherland, and Fiona Yarrow. "Paired Writing: A Framework of Effective Collaboration." *Literacy* 34, no. 2 (2000): 51–98. https://doi.org/10.1111/1467-9345.00139.

Topping, Keith. "Peer Assessment between Students in Colleges and Universities." *Review of Educational Research* 68, no. 3 (1998): 249–276. https://doi.org/10.2307/1170598.

Williams, Tracy. "Exploring the Impact of Study Abroad on Students' Intercultural Communication Skills: Adaptability and Sensitivity." *Journal of Studies in International Education* 9, no. 4 (2005): 356–371. https://doi.org/10.1177/1028315305277681.

CHAPTER 17

# English & Cultural Diversity: A Website for Teaching English as a World Language

*Bridget van de Grootevheen*

1 Introduction

The aim of this paper is to present EFL sample lessons with an intercultural focus.[1] Using these lessons, Dutch students in upper secondary school can study English and at the same time develop an understanding of identity and diversity issues through a multicultural and multilingual perspective. First, the current situation of the Dutch educational system will be discussed. Then literature from different disciplines will be reviewed and combined to contextualize the lessons. The disciplines involved are developmental psychology (Siegler et al. 2017; Feldman 2013), linguistics (Cole and Meadows 2013; Hall 2013), educational theories (Geerts and Van Kralingen 2016; Biggs and Tang 2011) and educational design principles (Van den Akker 2013). Finally, a critical look will be taken at the future of teaching intercultural communication in the Netherlands. The project can be positioned within the transfer approach to intercultural communication (Ten Thije 2020) as part of the curriculum for English as a foreign language has been re-designed to include intercultural communication. Thus Dutch students analyze materials that encourage transfer of intercultural competences and attitudes. The skills are transferred by means of Critical Discourse Analysis (CDA) (Cole and Meadows 2013).

2 The Dutch Education System and What Is about to Change

At the time of writing, the last revision of the Dutch curriculum was in 2006, so 16 years ago, when the Dutch government set core objectives and final standards. Due to the freedom of education, every school is allowed to design their own curriculum, as long as the government final objectives and standards are

---

1 This chapter is based on my MA thesis (Utrecht University 2020). The resultant website with assignments, answer keys, instructions for teachers and additional materials can be found at http://sites.google.com/view/englishandculturaldiversity/homepage

met. Nevertheless, a few advisory bodies have taken up the task of curriculum design and act as authorities in the Dutch school system, which has resulted in the creation of a relatively standardized curriculum. The main body is called SLO (*Stichting Leerplan Ontwikkeling*, Institute for Curriculum Development), a foundation responsible for shaping the objectives and standards into solid and concrete plans and advice. Then there is the KNAW (*Koninklijke Nederlandse Akademie van Wetenschappen*, Royal Dutch Academy of Sciences), a scientific institution that publishes high quality advice in the form of reports for all scientific disciplines and for society in general. In 2018, curriculum.nu (curriculum now) was founded as the main advisory body with the goal to revise the current curriculum. This body consists of nine development teams, in which teachers and school boards are represented in order to take a bottom-up approach. In 2023 some schools will start with pilots of the proposed curriculum. Not until 2026–2027 will the curriculum to be fully implemented and passed into legislation. The present study was designed to show how a recommendation by curriculum.nu on multilingualism (see below) could be implemented in upper-secondary English class in the Netherlands. Also, though curriculum.nu is the main responsible body, it is paradoxically not widely known among teachers. Hence, this study sought to incorporate their vision into freely available teaching materials.

The focus of the present research is on upper-secondary school HAVO and VWO students, in years 4–6 respectively. Upper secondary school starts in year 4. HAVO lasts 5 years in total and VWO 6 years. HAVO is senior general secondary education, which prepares students for higher professional education. VWO is pre-university education and prepares students for university. HAVO year 5 is about the same difficulty level as VWO year 4. Then there is also VMBO, which lasts 4 years and prepares students for vocational education. These three streams make up the secondary school system in the Netherlands.

In this system, Dutch and English are obligatory subjects for HAVO and VWO students for the entire period. Generally speaking, but depending on the school, French is introduced in the first year, and German in the second year. These are compulsory for the first three (or year 2 and 3) years of secondary school. HAVO students can drop both after 3 years, or continue with one or both for their exams. VWO students have to take at least one for their exams. Other languages that students can follow are Spanish, which is most widely available throughout the country, Italian, Turkish, Russian, Arabic, Chinese, Japanese, and Frisian, with the last six being generally speaking only available in a handful of schools, mostly located in larger cities. Students cannot take their exams in Japanese, and though Chinese is taught to HAVO students as well, the exams remain limited to VWO students. Within VWO, there are actually two streams.

In one of these, gymnasium, Latin and Old Greek are obligatory for the first three years of secondary school, and then students have to pick one or both of them for their final exams. The other stream, atheneum, also prepares students for university, but without necessarily studying Latin or Old Greek. There have been small-scale projects to make Latin and Old Greek available for VWO atheneum and HAVO students as well, but generally it remains exclusive to VWO gymnasium. Since 2018 the committee curriculum.nu has been drafting proposals for each subject. This time, intercultural communication is being incorporated into the curriculum. According to the KNAW (2018), more facilities and materials for language study are needed, and English as a subject should be kept from overshadowing other languages studied in the Netherlands.

Yet as English is spoken by many different cultural groups officially or non-officially, it could prove a fruitful way into multiculturality, multilingualism and diversity. English need not be limited to the UK and the US only, as it traditionally has been in English second language education in the Netherlands. Adopting a more inclusive approach to English might rid it of the negative connotation of overshadowing other languages and cultures if done carefully with current theoretical underpinnings and a solid strategy. That is exactly what this research set out to do. The starting point was expanding a recommendation made by curriculum.nu. This broadened the definition of multilingualism in the recommendation below by curriculum.nu from multiple languages and cultures to include linguistic varieties and a diversity of cultures *within the English language spectrum*: "Invite students to analyze the status and *use of languages and varieties in different countries and regions* [my emphasis] in a historical and socio-cultural perspective, in order to explain the values that are associated with them and to recognize stereotypes and prejudices and to ask critical questions about this."[2] The KNAW supports the view that language is the carrier of culture. English happens to be the carrier of many cultures worldwide and has a large body of varieties. Understanding these cultures through English enriches our understanding of the complex society we live in. This view of languages and cultures is especially suited for English education as it conveys and touches with multiple cultures and many other languages. Also, as it is a mandatory school subject in the Netherlands and the researcher was trained as an English teacher, it is the most practical way to reach as many upper-secondary school students as possible. It is an opportunity to have students reflect on their own identity, and diversity around them, through EFL education. Above all, it equips students with the necessary skills for the multilingual and multicul-

---

2 My translation, source: curriculum.nu, EMVT5.1—Meertaligheid—Aanbevelingen Bovenbouw VO.

tural society the KNAW recognizes we live in. To address these issues in language education, this project set out to investigate what assignments need to be developed to aid adolescents in upper-secondary school to form their identity through English as a foreign language (EFL) education.[3] In order to create these assignments, this project combined insights from developmental psychology, linguistics and educational theories to create assignments for students to educate them about cultural and linguistic diversity through English as a world language in the context of citizenship education. These insights combine Bronfenbrenner's bioecological mode of development; Kohlberg's Theory of Moral Reasoning; prosocial-moral dilemmas; different linguistic categorizations of *language*; Critical Discourse Analysis (CDA); Bloom's taxonomy; the curricular spider's web; and constructive alignment.[4] The design process consisted of three cycles, based on Van den Akker (2013), in which the assignments were built and then reviewed by both students and curriculum.nu developers.

## 3  Interculturality in English Classes Seen from Different Disciplines

The present study was designed to determine how one recommendation made by curriculum.nu on multilingualism below could be implemented in upper-secondary English class in the Netherlands. Central to the design of these assignments were educational design research and Critical Discourse Analysis (CDA) (Van den Akker 2013; Cole and Meadows 2013). Van den Akker (2013) identifies the problem of a disconnection between curriculum development and evidence-based research, in response to which the present paper founds the creation of assignments in these types of research. In practice, this meant that a design cycle was used to build the assignments through three iterative design phases. Educational theory (Biggs and Tang 2011; Geerts and Van Kralingen 2016) was also consulted to make sure the assignments function properly and are interconnected. The curricular spider's web (Van den Akker 2013) was used to support the objectives for each assignment and to ensure alignment. This is crucial to lesson materials because their constituent aspects are interconnected and interdependent.

---

3  Original research question: "What assignments need to be developed to aid adolescents in upper-secondary school to form their identity through English as a foreign language (EFL) education?"
4  Some of these are briefly discussed in section 3. For a full-length discussion, please consult my master's thesis (Van de Grootevheen 2020).

Critical Discourse Analysis was then used as an instrument to put the curriculum.nu recommendation into action, thereby providing concrete ways to transfer intercultural communication skills to the students. CDA is used to uncover common sense ideological components of texts and to put the perpetuation of these into perspective. These ideologies can be diverse in nature, for example nationalistic, linguistic, social, or cultural. CDA can also show the differences between practice and ideology and how the meaning-making processes in sociolinguistic situations are structured. For example, students can use CDA for a comparative analysis of the same statement in different contexts over time (Cole and Meadows 2013). CDA also uncovers the construction of human groups into 'us' and 'them.' Through the deconstruction of discourse students can disrupt the common sense that is part of it and ask critical questions about society. As conventional practice may be shaped by nationalist essentialist ideologies in the language classroom, it is important to equip students with CDA to counter this. Cole and Meadows (2013) define this essentialist trap as the belief that every nation is different, and that within each nation everyone is similar. It also includes the notion of tying one language to one country. When students focus on 'non-standard' or 'non-native' varieties, they develop flexibility in their language studies in the sense that they are more open to these varieties. For example, when Dutch students practice listening to Scottish English, they become more open to people speaking that variety instead of only tuning into American English (from television) and British English (at school). Because they have taken the time to understand the accent, they are less likely to judge people speaking it or waive it away with the excuse they do not understand. Moreover, by using Critical Discourse Analysis (CDA) students can establish a plurilithic view on languages, as CDA has proved a useful tool for analyzing linguistic varieties and cultural diversity.

Cole and Meadows (2013) define three ways in which nationalist essentialist discourse is constructed in the language classroom, and how the same three aspects can help deconstruct this by showing the variety that is inherent to any language. They are identified as follows:

- *Objectification.* Through objectification phenomena can be decontextualized and the attention can be restricted to a specific form. Language and cultural objects can be promoted as objects, and thus prescribed. For example, students can be asked to read out a poem in several dialects to highlight intonation and phonetic variation, linking these to well-known sociocultural personas (Cole & Meadows 2013).
- *Prescription.* Prescription is defining what is considered legitimate language, from a position of those having authority. Prescription is subject to sociopolitical struggle and privileges certain objects, thereby developing speakers'

disposition towards them. For example, a non-standard variety could be prescribed by reading out the poem from the aforementioned example in a formal situation, such as at a school or at a university.
- *Alignment.* Alignment is the selective linking of linguistic, cultural, and geographic variables to create and maintain sociolinguistic categories. It is picking those variables and forming them into a category that links a language to a social group, such as subcultures or ethnicities. Students can be informed on how to align with different identities and locations at different times, according to their wants and needs. For example, rather than presenting General American as a nationalized imagined ideal, when reading out a poem a teacher could align with a multitude of American accents from various regions in a way that "denaturalizes nationalist standard and its accompanying ideologies" (Cole and Meadows 2013, 41).

CDA can thus be used to highlight common sense ideologies, languages, and cultures or offer alternatives. Through these processes, linguistic diversity can combat the essentialist trap and offer students new perspectives on their identity and their role in society by putting (dominant) language and culture into perspective and challenge the status quo. CDA and its three aspects inform the ideas and method underlying each assignment on the website. Objectification, prescription and alignment are all part of CDA, and provide structure to help reach the set aims.

## 4   The Design and the Assignments

To create consistency, all assignments were laid out in the same way. They have clear objectives, start off with a presentation of the material, followed by exercises. Each assignment concludes with a reflection. All assignments have instructions for the teacher, an answer key, and if necessary extra materials to support the exercises.

The research process was focussed on finding suitable materials and devising tools to analyse them and use them in assignments. The teacher instructions that were added in the third iteration served to cater to the feedback provided by the curriculum developers. They identified the limitation that they would like to see the assignment in a classroom framework with suitable didactic methods and activities, which was likely to be mentioned by teachers as well. While the teacher instructions now provide indications of level, time, connections to other subject areas, and suggestions for teaching, they are not fully developed lesson plans. There are multiple reasons behind this decision. The idea behind creating the assignments was to take away the burden of seeking

TABLE 17.1   Assignments in the second iteration, including order of difficulty and logical order. Type indicates what material the assignment is based on. Keys were coded.

| Order | Assignment | Type | Key name |
|---|---|---|---|
| 1 | Tim Doner | A video clip and maps | KEY_1_TD |
| 2 | Windrush Child | Two poems by John Agard supported by videos and background texts | KEY_2_WC |
| 3 | Listen Mr. Oxford don | | KEY_3_LMOD |
| 4 | Foil Arms and Hog | Two comedy sketches | KEY_4_FAH |
| 5 | You Know What I'm Sayin'? | Two poems and a TED Talk by Daniel García Ordaz | KEY_5_YKWIS |
| 6 | Securing The Blessings | | KEY_6_STB |
| 7 | In Colorado My Father Scoured and Stacked Dishes | Poem with supporting video by Eduardo C. Corral | KEY_7_ECC |

out suitable materials for teachers, and to facilitate them with tools to analyze the materials. The assignments also needed to be adaptable to different levels, students, schedules, school cultures and teachers' own preferences. The website serves as a platform to facilitate teaching and to instigate discussion, not to take away the craftsmanship of the teacher. Since the assignments are fully supported with introductions, questions and keys, motivated and/or excellent students are able to work with the materials by themselves. Thereby the website offers differentiation for teachers as well as new perspectives for students outside of what they normally discuss in class. While it would answer the needs of the proposed curriculum to adapt these assignments into a classroom environment, it seemed preferable to make them available sooner rather than later for students and teachers to work with because waiting until everything is formally implemented would take away opportunities for students to learn about and deal with linguistic and cultural diversity. The loose nature of the assignments also promotes their adaptation into more project-based learning structures.

Table 17.1 provides an overview of the assignments and answer keys.

In a nutshell, assignment one regards multilingualism and discusses the stereotype of Americans only speaking English. The second and third assignment are about immigration from the Caribbean to the UK and about Jamaican

English. In assignment 4, Irish English vocabulary and Irish sarcasm are prescribed and objectified. Students are also aligned with Irish culture. In assignment 5 and 6 students align with American culture and with minorities through aligning with their history and by putting themselves in other people's shoes using spoken word poetry. The fifth assignment is about spoken word poetry and mimicking people in order to understand them better. The sixth assignment is about voting rights for African Americans and Mexican Americans in the United States. In assignment 7, the point is made not to privilege one language over another (English over Spanish) so that code-switching is prescribed while students learn to align with Mexican-American (illegal) immigrants. It is recommended to read through the website carefully to gain a more in-depth understanding of the assignments. All the materials for the assignments are available online, except for assignment five and six. Assignments 2 and 3 are connected through the use of two poems by the same author on a shared topic: immigration. Assignments 5 and 6 are connected in the same way through the shared topics citizenship and civil rights. While assignment 3 depends partly on 2, assignment 5 and 6 can be done separately. To clarify, assignments 7 and 4 will be presented here with their application of Critical Discourse Analysis.

### 4.1 *In Colorado My Father Scoured and Stacked Dishes: Code Switching*

As the assignments go up in number, the difficulty level increases, meaning 7 is most suited for grade 5 or 6 VWO students. The title is copied from the poem with the same name by Eduardo C. Corral, and "Code-switching" was added to indicate the focus. In this assignment students are introduced to Border Studies through the analysis of English-Spanish code-switching. Students learn about Border Studies, a field of study that is concerned with borders between people, such as the Mexican-American border. Students listen to the author reading his poem, in which he code-switches between English and Spanish. Then they analyze the poem on the significance of code-switching and encounter Mexican-American immigrant culture around the Mexican-American border. Finally they reflect on the way in which code-switching influences identity and connect this to Border Studies (Van de Grootevheen 2020). Through the analysis of the poem, students align with Mexican-American immigrant culture. More generally, they align with the child of an immigrant, who is the speaker of the poem. Code-switching is objectified and prescribed through reflecting on a statement the poet makes at the beginning of his speech. He states: "The Spanish is never italicized, put in context, there's no glossary. You know, if language is one way of viewing the world, I refuse to privilege one way of viewing over another." Students are then asked to reflect on the following questions: 1) How could this be representative of Border culture around the Mexican-American border? 2) What message would it give if the Spanish were actually italicized, put into context or in a glossary? 3) What dimensions does the Spanish add to the poem? Consider what it would be like if the poem was only in English. These questions describe code-switching as something positive and legitimate. Question 4 then asks students to suggest examples of global English usage, after which questions 5 and 6 lead students to alignment with the father of the speaker. Line 22 reads, "he strummed a guitarra, sang corridos. Arriba" and students are asked why it matters that here the word "corridos" is used, and how it differs from 'songs.' Lines 27–28 read, "once, like a window. ¡No mames! His favorite / belt buckle: an águila perched on a nopal." It is clarified for the students that the belt buckle is a reference to the coat of arms of Mexico, and they are asked what this says about the father's identity. Finally, students reflect on the influence of code-switching on identity, on the advantages code-switching offers, and relate these questions to their own experiences, the poem and Border Studies.

### 4.2 Foil Arms and Hog

Foil Arms and Hog is an Irish sketch comedy group, and in this assignment, students watch and analyze two of their sketches, one on Irish Gaelic (known as Irish) and one on Irish English. First, they read about the history of Irish Gaelic and Irish English to understand the background of the comedy sketches. Then they watch one sketch about a questioning by the police in which the ability to speak Irish English is made into a joke. They have to try to find a connection between the comedy sketch and the values that are associated with Irish. Then they watch another sketch in which Irish English vocabulary and sarcasm cause a misunderstanding between two speakers of English (Irish English and Standard English) in a business context. They have to try to solve the misunderstanding. In the end, they reflect on the value their own language or language variety has in society (Van de Grootevheen 2020). So in this assignment, Irish and Irish English are objectified and prescribed. Students have to critically look at the stereotypes associated with them and actively debunk those stereotypes. They have to actively think about the values that speaking Irish and/or Irish English brings and connect this to the values associated to their own language use. In the first sketch, in which a suspect from an Irish speaking region (Connemara) in Ireland is questioned by the police, who do not speak Irish much, students also have to align with the suspect. They imagine they are from Connemara, and answer the following question: "What do you think of the importance of the Irish language to be represented in official institutions, such as the police or in court?" (Van de Grootevheen 2020). On the other hand, they also have to think from the perspective of the police and decide why it is important to speak at least a little bit of Irish in Ireland, rather than only knowing swearwords. In the second sketch, students have to align with both parties, namely an administrator from the European office, and the person in charge of the Irish branch of a firm. They come up with strategies to negotiate and accommodate in the discussion between these two people, in order to create an environment in which both sides try to come closer and clarify their language use and expectations. This way students do not focus on misunderstanding per se, as is unfortunately often the case in intercultural communication research, but rather on going beyond misunderstanding and thereby focusing on mutual understanding (Messelink and Ten Thije 2012). In the reflection, students objectify and prescribe their own language variety. They are asked to use positive and negative stereotypes to describe the status of their variety, while highlighting where these stereotypes come from and how they influence the position of the language in question (Van de Grootevheen 2020).

## 5  Conclusion and Discussion

The present study set out to develop assignments for EFL class for upper-secondary students in the Netherlands, so that English teachers have something to work with and not have to wait until the implementation of the new curriculum. Giving intercultural communication a spot in the curriculum should be done sooner rather than later. To this end, the project has provided a deeper insight into the combination of psychological, linguistic, cultural and educational research into forming well-rounded products that can be used by teachers and students. Moreover, Critical Discourse Analysis was used as an instrument to transfer intercultural competences to the students. Consultation with students and curriculum.nu developers showed that the designed materials offer an effective implementation of the recommendations of curriculum.nu. Since multilingualism is a new aspect of foreign language education in the Netherlands, this study stretched the definition of multilingualism used by curriculum.nu from the notion of multiple languages and cultures, to include linguistic varieties of the same language, English, to express different cultures. The assignments that were created successfully reflect this. After the project was finished in July 2020, the materials were included on the taalwijs.nu website in October 2020. Taalwijs.nu is a website where language teachers in secondary education, teacher trainers and university language specialists meet. It is an initiative of the National Platform for Languages, which is committed to renewing language education and improving the connection between secondary and higher education in the Netherlands. This was valuable to the project, as it is much easier to find the project this way and reaches a larger and wider audience than the original website. This way, teachers and students do not have to wait until 2026–2027 and can just start using the assignments right away. It visualizes the possibilities of incorporating intercultural communication in the curriculum and encourages more people to take it up and design materials, as many more will be needed, even before the 2023 pilot.

A limitation of the project is that the website was created free with a sites.google.com domain, and with complete disregard to marketing and SEO. This makes it nearly impossible to find the original website just by typing in the name in a search bar, save from a link on the researcher's LinkedIn page. Therefore, the researcher plans to move the website and make it easier to find on the web. Another limitation of the study is that since the assignments were created in isolation from the classroom, discussion and interaction on the subject matter was not possible. Individual students found the assignments quite challenging and would have benefitted from a classroom environment with a teacher to coach them, which would also reduce the time it takes to complete each assignment. On the other hand, because of the COVID-19 outbreak, it was difficult or impossible for teachers to aid their students in making the pilot assignments. For this reason, and maybe because they had online classes all day, students may have been less motivated to put in the extra effort some of these assignments need. That being said, materials that serve as aids were created during the design process, for example longer instructions and keys. Also, more resources were added in individual assignments to encourage independent completion. In the last iteration, resources for teachers were also added to facilitate adaptation of assignments to a classroom environment. In general, therefore, it seems that the design process was influenced by desired guidance by students and desired classroom adaptability by curriculum.nu developers. This resulted in high quality content, suited for independent use, but also in flexibility meeting teachers' needs.

The educational design process in this study has been one of the first attempts to thoroughly examine the implications of curriculum.nu suggestions. This interdisciplinary design approach will prove useful in expanding our understanding of how more linguistically and culturally diverse content can be implemented in the English curriculum in the Netherlands. A limitation to this design process, however, is that it is rather complex and is more suited for a long-term study that goes through more than just three cycles. Educational design research should include multiple testing phases in a classroom environment. It is also unfortunate that this study did not include languages other than English, as multilingualism was within English language varieties. Therefore, this study does not entirely do justice to promoting multilingualism as it is restricted to the English language classroom. Also, the generalizability of the results in this study is subject to certain limitations. For instance, the students were in an uncontrolled situation at home. They were not available for follow-up questions. The assignments were also not tested in a classroom situation, so it remains unknown what limitations could come up in that setting. Moreover, the materials offer a great opportunity to discuss identity and diversity and would allow students to share their stories with each other. Another limitation regarding generalisability of the results is that teachers did not provide feedback. If they had, the design process would have reflected their thoughts and ideas on the assignments as well and consequently the assignments might have come out quite differently.

Despite the promising results, opportunities that require further investigation remain. For example, there is still a wealth of resources waiting to be adapted into assignments, resources that similar to the ones in this assignment are uncommon in the present school-system, meaning they diverge from 'native-speakerism' British and American English content that is overly present in Dutch classrooms. There are many more resources for students to encounter non-standard varieties and different cultures. In addition, further collaboration could be reached between the languages taught in Dutch secondary schools, mainly Dutch, French, German and Spanish. Moreover, connections could be made to languages that students may speak at home such as Arabic, Turkish, Tamazight (Berber), and Polish. Attempts were already successfully made in the assignments by analysing English-Spanish code-switching and having students reflect on their home languages. Future assignments could be designed in further collaboration with both schools and curriculum.nu to ensure these topics are included in school environments. Continued efforts are needed to make linguistic and cultural diversity more visible in the curricula at Dutch schools. A key policy priority should therefore be to develop the long-term plans for multilingualism at a cross-curricular level. German, French, Spanish and other foreign language students enrolled in teacher training could take up this research and cooperate and contribute to the current website to broaden the platform. They can also collaborate on assignments and teach those to students on a cross-curricular level. The possibilities are endless.

### References

Akker, Jan van den. "Curricular Development Research as a Specimen of Educational Design Research." In *Educational Design Research Part A: An Introduction*, edited by

Tjeerd Plomp and Nienke Nieveen, 52–71. Enschede: SLO, 2013.

Biggs, John, and Catherine Tang. *Teaching for Quality Learning at University: What the student does (3rd ed.)*. New York: McGraw-Hill Education, 2011.

Cole, Debbie, and Brian Meadows. "Avoiding the Essentialist Trap in Intercultural Education: Using Critical Discourse Analysis to Read Nationalist Ideologies in the Language Classroom." *Linguistics for Intercultural Education* 33 (2013): 29–47.

Feldman, Robert S. *Ontwikkelingspsychologie: 5$^e$ editie*. Amsterdam: Pearson Benelux B.V, 2012.

Geerts, Walter, and René van Kralingen. *Handboek voor Leraren*. Bussum: Coutinho, 2016.

Grootevheen, Bridget van de. "English & Cultural Diversity: Identity Formation in Adolescence through the Analysis of Linguistic and Cultural Diversity." Master's thesis, Utrecht University, 2020.

Grootevheen, Bridget van de. "English and Cultural Diversity." 2020. https://sites.google.com/view/englishandculturaldiversity/homepage.

Hall, Christopher. "Cognitive Contributions to Plurilithic Views of English and Other Languages." *Applied Linguistics*, 34, no. 2 (2013): 211–223.

Messelink, Annelies, and Jan D. ten Thije. "Unity in Super-diversity: European Capacity and Intercultural Inquisitiveness of the Erasmus Generation 2.0." *Dutch Journal for Applied Linguistics (DuJAL)* 1 (2012): 81–101.

Siegler, Robert, Nancy Eisenberg, Elizabeth Gershoff, Judy R., Saffran, Jenny, DeLoache, and Campbell Leaper. *How Children Develop: 5th edition*. New York: Worth Publishers, 2017.

"Talen voor Nederland." KNAW. 2018. https://knaw.nl/nl/actueel/publicaties/talen-voor-nederland.

Thije, Jan D. ten. "What Is Intercultural Communication." In *The Cambridge Handbook of Intercultural Communication*, edited by Guido Rings and Sebastian Rasinger. Cambridge: Cambridge University Press, 2020.

"De voorstellen: Engels/MVT." Curriculum. 2019. https://www.curriculum.nu/voorstellen/engels-mvt/.

CHAPTER 18

# Intercultural Ethnographies of Students Abroad: International Experience Becomes Intercultural Learning

*Jana Untiedt and Annelies Messelink*

## 1   Introduction

Internationalization is on the daily agenda of universities worldwide (Zhu 2013). One of the main contributions to internationalization is student mobility with an ever-increasing number of students deciding to study abroad (ICEF 2015). The primary goal of studying abroad is often gaining intercultural competence (Salisbury, Ann and Pascarella 2013). Participating in a study abroad program can bring advantages, such as intercultural competence (Relyea, Cocchiara and Studdard 2008), personal development, improved language skills (Burns and Novelli 2008) and even management skills (Van 't Kloster, van Wijk and van Rekom 2009).

While mobility is indeed greatly promoted as a means of personal and even professional development, Vande Berg, Connor-Linton and Paige (2009) state this belief can be misleading. In fact, intercultural contact and experience in themselves do not guarantee intercultural learning (Deardorff 2006; IEREST 2015; Vande Berg, Connor-Linton and Paige 2009) and can potentially even reinforce stereotypes, prejudice and racism (Allport 1954; Deardorff 2004). Furthermore, students can experience practical barriers (e.g., immigration, bureaucratic matters) and emotional challenges such as culture shock, (e.g., integration, homesickness, cf. Esser 2010, in Nazarkiewicz and Kraemer 2012), identity crises (ibid.) and re-entry culture shocks upon return (Gaw 2002) which can diminish the positive impact of an international experience. In addition, Messelink, Van Maele and Spencer-Oatey (2015) suggest that students are not always aware of what they learn from their intercultural experience, or able to formulate this in relevant ways.

In order to enhance the positive outcomes of a mobility experience, Vande Berg and Paige (2012) claim the experience should be integrated in the curriculum. Through intercultural training and guidance, students learn to better reflect on intercultural topics and become more culturally aware. Through the use of cultural mentors and interventions, negative experiences of students can be reflected upon or even diminished (Vande Berg and Paige 2012). With guidance, students can learn to deconstruct stereotypes, gain self-awareness and make a better self-estimation of the needed skills (Deardorff 2006). Finally, when helped to verbalize their experience, students become more aware of their learnings abroad and learn to capitalize on this experience.

Brewer and Solberg (2009) state that universities generally fail to see that intercultural learning can be enhanced through training and guidance. According to them, the support of sending and host universities often focuses only on practical matters, such as logistics, course itineraries and language classes and rarely on preparations for the target culture and language, or, more generally, for cultural adjustment. This lack of preparation leads to students arriving unprepared in host countries and therefore to a more limited learning experience (Brewer and Solberg 2009). In fact, returning students sometimes feel they did not achieve or learn as much from the experience as they had expected (Zemach-Birsin 2008 as cited in Berg, Paige and Lou 2012), as such leaving potential untapped. In order to maximize the learning effect, Vande Berg and Paige (2012) stress that education and guidance should not merely occur before the experience, but also during and after students' stay abroad. This consideration provided the basis for a university course offered by Utrecht University, which will be discussed in the next section.

## 2   The Intercultural Learning Course

During the second semester of 2015, Utrecht University organized a pilot course Intercultural Learning for outgoing Dutch students. The second author, and teacher of this course, adopted a non-essentialist approach, which emphasizes that culture is dynamic, identities are multifaceted and meaning is jointly constructed in interaction (cf. Holliday 2010; Van Maele and Messelink, 2019). The course partly made use of intercultural education resources for Erasmus students, developed in the IEREST-project (2015), funded within the Lifelong Learning Programme. The course consisted of the three modules listed in Table 18.1.

While all three modules aim to contribute to intercultural learning, the second module provided the core for this paper's analysis. In this module, all students wrote at least two out of three ethnographies, reflecting on their social, academic and cultural life abroad. Most ethnographies discussed in this paper are from assignments one and three (social and cultural life). The ethnographies and corresponding topics will be discussed in more detail in the methodology section. We will first review authors and theories which stress the relevance of reflection on intercultural learning.

TABLE 18.1  Overview of modules of pilot course "Intercultural Training"

| Module | Timing | Content | Purpose |
|---|---|---|---|
| 1 | took place before departure | – Basic notions of culture and identities<br>– Concepts such as self and other by investigating student blogs about students' destination | prepare and manage expectations of study abroad experience |
| 2 | during stay abroad | – Writing three intercultural ethnographies on three themes (social, academic and cultural life)<br>– an online mini-lecture and literature on mobility and interculturality to help students understand and describe learning experiences | stimulating critical reflection on students' real-life encounters and experiences abroad |
| 3 | after return | – one session for students to discuss their experiences by using the W-curve (Gullahorn & Gullahorn, 1963), how stay changes them and discussing the re-entry phase<br>– one career training in collaboration with Career Services with a focus on verbalizing new or enhanced skills | capitalizing on experiences by reframing them for narratives of personal and professional capacities |

## 3   Learning and Changing through Intercultural Contact

As indicated above, intercultural contact in itself does not guarantee learning (Deardorff 2006). According to many authors, most learning takes place through critically reflecting on one's experience. Therefore, reflecting on intercultural interactions is crucial for learning (Zhu 2016; Passarelli and Kolb 2012; Vande Berg and Paige 2012; Thomas 2006). A theory supporting this insight is the educational experiential learning theory of Kolb (1984), exploring four phases of a learning cycle. The first phase consists of a *concrete experience*. In the second phase this experience is *observed and reflected upon*. This reflection can lead to *conceptualizations* and new ideas or actualizations of an abstract concept (e.g., acquiring or updating cultural knowledge). In the fourth experimentation phase, learners apply this new knowledge and test their conceptualizations in real life, (e.g., testing to what extent a 'cultural rule' appears accurate and applicable to different contexts). This last phase can often restart the cycle, which leads to fine-tuning the (intercultural) learning process.

A crucial guideline for intercultural educators is to stimulate reflection on concrete intercultural experiences to enhance experiential learning. One way to do this is to have students document their intercultural experiences and their related thoughts and feelings in reflective learning journals or intercultural ethnographies (Holmes and O'Neill 2012). Students take on the role of a participatory observant, corresponding to the more traditional methodology of an ethnography (Jordan 2002). Educators can help students better understand the personal and intercultural aspects of their encounters by providing feedback and asking deeper questions. Intercultural ethnographies allow students insight into their own development and learning process, while also making intercultural learning visible and comprehensible for teachers (Holmes and O'Neill 2012). Through intercultural ethnographies students learn to critically evaluate their own cultural assumptions and behavioral patterns. These reflection processes can lead to an increase in cultural self-awareness (Deardorff 2006; Byram 1997), but can also result in changes in one's perspective according to the transformative learning theory (Mezirow 1997). Mezirow (1997) explains that learning is a process in which assumptions, expectations or interpretations of events are compared to interpretations made earlier. This can lead to newly constructed or revised interpretations which inevitably leads to a paradigmatic shift in an individual's reference frame. When students consider different perspectives and question their own cultural assumptions (Vande Berg and Paige 2012), transformations can occur in their knowledge, attitude and behavior (Perry and Southwell 2011; Deardorff 2006; Mezirow 1997). The result is a more inclusive, differentiated and more critically reflective reference frame (Mezirow 1997). The ability to switch from and collect new reference frames and ways of thinking is crucial when interacting with individuals from other cultural backgrounds where different perspectives are often represented. According to Deardorff (2006), this increases students' empathy, ethnorelativity and adaptability, highlighting the importance of reflection for intercultural growth. In fact, the ability to *learn* and *change* through intercultural *contact* can be considered as a crucial intercultural competence.

Kim's (2001) stress-adaptation-growth model also helps explain how individuals learn from intercultural contact and how this ultimately changes them and their views. According to Kim (2001), when we encounter individuals with different values, norms and behavior, we experience stress. As a result, we become uncertain whether we can maintain our own (cultural) values or whether we should change our behavior to establish security. This can lead to changes in behavior when individuals try to cope and reduce conflict by acquiring new practices (acculturation) or leaving former cultural practices behind (deculturation). Ultimately, Kim (2008) speaks of an "intercultural evolution" where cumulative intercultural experiences can lead to changes in the individual. Students may also encounter various stress factors abroad (Paige 1993), related to personal and cultural issues. By providing proper guidance in these situations and enabling students to critically reflect on their own and others' perspectives, educators can greatly stimulate personal and intercultural growth.

## 4 Methodology

This study uses directed (DCA) and conventional content analysis (CCA) to examine intercultural learning experiences in students' reflection reports. In directed content analysis, the categories used for analysis are based on existing theory (Hsieh and Shannon 2005) while in CCA, these categories are developed inductively during the analysis (Mayring 2000) and are purely derived from the research material (Kondracki and Wellman 2002). The analysis in this study is divided into four steps. First, all descriptions of intercultural experiences in the ethnographies were marked, since intercultural experience has been repetitively stressed as an important source for learning (Thomas 2006; Passarelli and Kolb 2012). This resulted in 128 text sections where intercultural experiences were mentioned. These text sections demonstrated high similarity with the learning phases of Kolb's (1984) experiential learning cycle. In the second phase these 128 text sections were re-coded according to Kolb's learning phases: *Experience, reflection, conceptualization* and *experimentation*. This DCA led to the identification of 690 text parts in which different learning phases occurred. As a third step, another CCA was conducted to examine the topics that students discussed in the 690 text parts. Here, it became evident that students repeatedly reported different techniques in dealing with and learning from intercultural encounters. This led to the fourth step of the analyses, in which three learning techniques were deduced: *comparison of the unfamiliar with the familiar, reflection on stereotypes* and *verification through third parties*. These will be further discussed in the result section.

### 4.1 Materials and Participants

The materials for this research consisted of 27 ethnographies. These ethnographies were written by 20 students as part of the second module of the course Intercultural Learning while they were abroad. Since participation in the course was voluntary, participants likely had an increased interest in cultures or intercultural learning. No credit points were awarded for participation, but students did receive a certificate upon completion of all training and after submitting at least two ethnographies. Out of all students, 85% were female and 15% were male. The average age of the students is unknown. All respondents had at least the Dutch nationality. As students from all faculties could apply for the course, fields of study were highly diverse, ranging from mathematics to geography to cultural anthropology (N=4), which increases the possibility of prior education in cultural topics. Out of all students, 85% studied abroad while 15% did an internship abroad. The average duration of their stays was 156 days (5.2 months), with one stay of unknown length. Each students' timeline differed with regard to departure and return date, as well as duration of stay abroad. The destinations were Europe (50%), Oceania (20%), North America (15%) and South-America (5%). Asia and Africa were not represented.

### 4.2  Two Assignments

In this paper, we will analyze the first and third assignment of the second module, which were presented either at the start or near the end of the students' stay abroad. The first assignment focused on students' social environment while the latter addressed students' perception of culture and communication. In the first ethnography, students reflected on their social network abroad as well as their contact with people at home, potential difficulties they experienced adapting to their new environment and to what extent they consulted locals, international students or co-nationals to overcome said difficulties. They were also asked to describe one intercultural encounter (critical incident) which had made an impact and to reflect on their own interpretation of this situation as well as hypothesize about the perspectives of other interactants. In the third assignment students reflected on experiences of stereotyping, essentializing and exotism. They contemplated to what extent they adapted certain behaviors and attitudes more or less easily and what they had learned about the host countries, other internationals and their own culture. They were again asked to critically reflect on one particular intercultural encounter (critical incident). Out of the 128 text sections that represented intercultural experiences, 62.5% of the analyzed text sections originated from the assignment about culture and communication. This is understandable as this assignment focused more on examples of actual intercultural encounters with local and international students and therefore was in line with the scope of this paper's analysis, to demonstrate how reflection on intercultural experience can enhance intercultural awareness and learning.

## 5 Results

In this section we first illustrate how all four *learning phases* (Kolb, 1984) occur in the students' ethnographies, with 5.2 focusing on the main three *learning techniques* that were identified during further analysis of each phase, and 5.3 demonstrating how the analysis of learning phases and learning techniques can also shed light on actual *learning outcomes*. We then conclude that intercultural ethnographies can be used to illustrate the learning process and learning outcomes of students. All examples are taken from Untiedt (2016).

### 5.1 *Learning Phases*

When taking a closer look at the 27 intercultural ethnographies, it becomes evident that students do undergo the four phases of Kolb's (1984) learning cycle (Table 18.2). This learning cycle was also discussed in the first assignments' mini-lecture.

TABLE 18.2  Overview of frequency of all 690 text parts that represented learning phases

| Phase | Experience | Reflection | Conceptualization | Experimentation |
|---|---|---|---|---|
| N | 251 | 255 | 147 | 37 |

Each text part included one or more phases of the learning cycle. The excerpt below includes all four phases of the learning cycle, where the last experimentation restarts the cycle from experience to experimentation.

> **Experience:** "When I had been here for a month [...] I saw a friend of mine approaching me from a distance. Once we stood in front of each other, I said hi and she responded: 'how are you?' Since I had experienced that asking this question mostly doesn't mean that the person asking is interested in the answer, I didn't find it worth reacting and I just continued walking (I was a bit busy) without answering."

In this fragment the student first describes repeated intercultural encounters where someone asked him "How are you?" (experience). This made him wonder about the fact that this question might not be an actual question in his host country, but mostly a form of small talk (reflection). This led him to the conceptualization that this "mostly doesn't mean that the person asking is interested in the answer." He then decides to experiment with not answering the question at all. This experimentation restarts the cycle as the student reflects on not answering:

> **Reflection:** "Thinking about it later, I thought that even though it might not be a sincere question, you are expected to answer."

The student conceptualizes that it is considered rude to not respond at all.

> **Conceptualization:** "That's why I think that it was very impolite of me to not respond to the question."

This led him to redefine his conceptualization and re-adjust his behavior to a brief response.

> **Experimentation:** "Now I always answer something between "relatively fine" or "fantastic"—never more than three words except for when we are really having a conversation—followed by "how are you?"

This fragment demonstrates how reflection on intercultural encounters can lead to the shaping of cultural understanding and, subsequently, altered behavior. The fragments demonstrate the recursive nature of the learning cycle, where experimentation of a conceptualization can lead to a new experience, which is then again reflected upon and potentially leads to a new conceptualization and the adjustment of behavior (experimentation). This recursiveness highlights that (intercultural) learning is a continuous process.

### 5.2    *Learning Techniques*

After analyzing the four learning phases in the 690 text parts, we identified three learning techniques that students regularly discussed in dealing with and learning from intercultural encounters. All three techniques were also mentioned in the assignments of the ethnographies. We will here analyze the use of techniques as reported by students and focus on the outcomes of using these techniques.

The first technique is *comparing the unfamiliar with the familiar*, where students compare their experiences abroad to what they are used to at home. This technique was displayed by 90% of the participants (N=18) and found in 81% of the reflection reports (N=22). These comparisons often overlapped with the conceptualization phase and demonstrated a shift in reference frame, as the following example illustrates:

But there are certainly other typical similarities and differences. I thought that the high environmental awareness and knowledge of climate change was interesting. People look at you with disgust if you are using too much plastic. [...] Something that is less common in the Netherlands [...] Through this I have learned about my own culture that [...] we can learn a lot from them

In this example, the student makes a comparison between environmental awareness in California and the Netherlands. By comparing the situation in California to the familiar context of the Netherlands, she first reflects on differences with regards to using plastic and then revises her own interpretation of environmental issues. In fact, she feels that people in the Netherlands can learn from the people in California. Therefore, by comparing the unfamiliar with the familiar the student is prompted to evaluate her individually and culturally determined perceptions and to revise earlier interpretations with new assumptions, expectations or interpretations (Mezirow 1997). This example shows how reflection on intercultural experiences can cause a change in reference frame (Deardorff 2006) which might also result in changes in her behavior. Another student also confirmed the value of this learning technique, comparing cultural events to familiar contexts, by referring to the mini lecture: "As you said in the lecture it can be helpful to think about the Netherlands."

The second learning technique *reflection on stereotypes* was described by 65% of participants (N=13) and was mentioned in 56% of reflection reports (N=15). In the last assignment, students were asked to write about images of the self and other, including generalizations and stereotypes, and whether some of their images had changed over time. These student reflections on their stereotypes of the host country or other international students led to different outcomes. Most students reported that their stereotypes were confirmed (32%, N=35), a quarter reported a rejection (25%, N=27) or just discussed stereotypes in general (14%, N=15). Some students also included reasons behind their stereotypes (25%, N=27) or tried to show different nuances of stereotypes (18%, N=20).

The final learning technique that was demonstrated by 35% (N=7) of all participants in 26% (N=7) of the ethnographies, is *third-party verification*. A mobility experience generally offers the opportunity to verify stereotypes, interpretations or conceptualizations about certain groups, with so-called representatives of these groups. In the assignment, students were encouraged to verify their conceptualizations with local or international students whenever possible. This sometimes led to more questions but also to the confirmation or rejection of beliefs. For example, one student reported another student leaving unannounced during a lecture, which the student interpreted as impolite. She verified this interpretation with another international student who felt the same. The student then asked a local student, who explained that students have to leave lectures earlier to attend overlapping lectures. After this explanation the student no longer felt the behavior was impolite and even started behaving the same way. This demonstrates that at first the student applied her own academic frame to the Austrian academic context. But, as is often the case in intercultural communication, these frames differ. By encouraging a student to *verify with third parties*, we encourage them to search for new reference frames from which interpretations can be made. In this way, verification can play a crucial role between the reflection and conceptualization phases of intercultural learning. Of course, 'locals' are not necessarily aware of underlying reasons for their behavior, nor do students always agree with their explanation, which means that third-party verification does not always result in a revised interpretation and therefore neither in a shift of reference frame.

### 5.3  *Learning Outcomes*

This section demonstrates how the analysis of both the learning phases of Kolb's cycle (1984) and the previously discussed learning techniques also provides insights in students' learning outcomes. We first analyzed how students acquire knowledge, either culture-specific (80%, N= 116), culture-general (7%, N= 10), or self-knowledge (13%, N= 18). Many times students tried to explain differences by conceptualizing certain cultural 'rules' and regularities. This occurred mostly during the conceptualization phase. In turn, these 'rules' were either accepted or rejected or led to new realizations and behaviors of the learner. There are many examples of students gaining *cultural-specific knowledge*, either referring to the host country, their own culture or cultures of fellow international students. For example, one student noticed that Australians use many abbreviations. Locals explained to her that abbreviations are easier to use. She then linked the usage of abbreviations to more informal atmosphere and conceptualized that "Australians do not like to be formal." Another student was surprised by how many students own a car in Aruba. Comparing this to the Netherlands, she realized that the Netherlands really is a "biking country." These examples demonstrate that students gained culture-specific knowledge, using different learning techniques (in this case, comparing and verifying).

In ten instances students displayed *culture-general knowledge*, demonstrating a more general and non-essential understanding of cultures. The following statement is an excellent example of how students acquired a more dynamic view on culture and identities (Holliday 2010):

> Before I went to Germany, I thought all Germans would be pragmatic and direct [...]. Even though they are direct and love rules, these are not the most important characteristics of the Germans I have met [...]. Thus, the stereotype is not true. I myself never had to experience stereotypes a lot. [...] I only remember a conversation with someone from Belgium that told me that Belgium had this image of Dutch people being direct. Meeting me, he saw this stereotype as confirmed, but not for every other Dutch person he had met. Based on the rejected stereotypes one can see that [...] differences between people are not a result of their origin, but more of their personality.

The student describes the partial rejection of his stereotype of Germans and stereotypes of others about Dutch people. The use of stereotypes for intercultural learning has been stressed by Allport (1954), who claims that the rejection of stereotypes leads to a more open attitude as individuals are less frequently seen as representatives of their own national culture. This is very clearly illustrated in this fragment, where the rejections of stereotypes lead to his conclusion that "everyone is different" and that differences are not caused by one's origin, but one's personality. The student thus demonstrates culture-general knowledge and a non-essentialist view on culture and identity. It indicates that new experiences can lead to a more inclusive and differentiated reference frame (Mezirow 1997).

In 18 instances students demonstrated increasing intercultural *self-knowledge* and awareness. In one example, a student complained about bike lanes in the host country, then is asked how this is handled in her home country and realizes that she does not actually know this and that she showed a "number-one mentality" (Agar 1995), meaning that she made a judgement about her host culture, assuming her own culture was better. This realization encouraged her to be more open minded about differences:

> I felt a bit uncomfortable, because I had just complained about the German way of handling this, whereas this probably isn't handled differently in the Netherlands. [...] it made me realize that I showed a number-one mentality: I assumed that everything in the Netherlands was better, whereas I myself didn't really know how it was handled in the Netherlands and what the difference was. From this, I have learned to have a more open-minded attitude.

Learning outcomes described in the experimentation learning phase mainly refer to changes in behavior. Students most frequently described instances of acculturation (62%, N=23), which means adjusting one's behavior or attitude to the host culture, or examples of deculturation (30% N=11), which means that they 'unlearned' behavior or attitudes corresponding to their own culture, while fewer students discussed how they actively maintained familiar habits (8%, N=3).

One example of acculturation is a student providing examples of experiences with Australians, which he feels are "incredibly friendly and helpful" and, after comparing them to Dutch people, "much more open." The student then describes how he adapted his behavior, for example by saying sorry or thank you more often. In eleven instances, students discussed examples of *deculturation* (30%, N=11). For example, one student moved in with ten American girls and constantly asked them about their activities during the day and their plans for the rest of the day. She explains that not asking these questions would be considered rude in the Netherlands and that she does this to demonstrate interest. However, when she came to realize that her American roommates found these questions intrusive and did not appreciate her behavior, the student changed her behavior and noticed that the interaction improved.

Students also described the maintenance of *familiar habits* (8%, N=3), which means they chose not to adapt to the host culture's ways of doing and thinking. For example, one student mentioned that her roommates do not socialize with other students. A local student explains that the roommates prefer being on their own after a social day. Even though the Dutch student now understood the reason for this behavior, she still decided to continue introducing herself and interacting with her fellow roommates, accepting that she might be seen as "that weird Dutch person."

During the experimentation phase, students clearly demonstrated the ability to choose whether or not to adapt to other ways of doing or thinking, in order to cope better with intercultural situations and to establish better relationships with others. They also demonstrated the ability to choose to not change their behavior. In fact, adaptation is not the main goal of intercultural learning. It is more important to become aware of one's own knowledge and attitudes, to be able to handle differences and to learn from intercultural interactions. This, then, does not minimize differences between cultures, but introduces new ways of understanding the world (reference frames) and undergoing an "intercultural evolution" (Kim 2008) where cumulative intercultural experience can actually change an individual.

## 5    Conclusion

This paper provided insight into the way in which intercultural ethnographies demonstrate students' intercultural learning. We analyzed 27 intercultural ethnographies of 20 Dutch students participating in an intercultural learning course guiding them before, during and after their study or internship abroad. Each student wrote two or three ethnographies in which they mostly reflected on their social and cultural life abroad. Using conventional content analysis, each description of an intercultural experiences was marked. Many descriptions appeared to coincide with one of Kolb's (1984) four phases of the experiential learning cycle (experience, reflection, conceptualization and experimentation). This suits the aim of an intercultural ethnography, namely to gain insight into one's own development and learning process (Holmes and O'Neill 2012). The first two phases *experience* and *reflection* occurred most often, which is not surprising as students were asked to describe an intercultural experience. We furthermore noticed that the experimentation phase often led to new experiences where students tested new conceptualizations in real life. This confirms that the experimentation phase can restart the entire learning cycle (Kolb 1984) and demonstrates that intercultural learning is an ongoing process.

The analysis of each learning phase demonstrated three learning techniques that students regularly applied in intercultural encounters. We subsequently analyzed the learning outcomes gained through the use of these techniques. Partly in the reflection and mostly in the conceptualization phase, students reflected on stereotypes and verified their interpretations with third parties. This enabled students to gain, adjust or verify their acquired culture-specific or culture-general knowledge. Students clearly demonstrated the ability to acquire and understand new perspectives (Allport 1954; Mezirow 1997; Deardorff 2006; 2009). Changes in behavior were also reported, most often in the experimentation learning phase. Students critically evaluated their own cultural assumptions, perceptions and behavioral patterns. Sometimes students preferred the perspectives of other cultures over the perspectives of their own, which was demonstrated in the learning technique *comparing the unfamiliar to the familiar*. Students provided clear illustrations of acculturation (acquiring new practices), deculturation (leaving old habits behind) and maintenance (deliberately not adapting one's behavior). Finally, the ethnographies demonstrate that students' notion of culture in general changed (e.g., Allport 1954; Kolb 1984; Deardorff 2006; 2009). Students realized that their own interpretations are culturally influenced. They reported the importance of being aware of one's expectations based on origin. Some also reported that individual characteristics are a stronger determinant of behavior than national origin.

We want to conclude by delineating two assumptions that were presented in the introduction. First, the analysis of ethnographies stresses that intercultural experience is an essential part of intercultural learning (Vande Berg and Paige 2012; Holmes and O'Neill 2012; Deardorff 2006; Zhu 2016; Passarelli and Kolb 2012; Thomas 2006; Kolb 1984; Mezirow 1997). Theory states that learning from intercultural contact is not a given and that it can be enhanced through intercultural training and guidance (Vande Berg and Paige 2012). The key for turning intercultural experiences into intercultural learning is reflection (Zhu 2016; Passarelli and Kolb 2012; Thomas 2006; Vande Berg and Paige 2012) and learning increases when students are aware of their own learning experience (Deardorff 2006). This is in fact the aim of intercultural ethnographies, namely to allow students to gain insight into their own development and learning process and to make learning and growth visible and comprehensible to students and others (Holmes and O'Neill 2012). The analysis of these ethnographies demonstrated changes in students' perspectives, attitudes and behavior (Mezirow 1997; Kim 2001; Kolb 1984; Deardorff 2006; 2009). It affirms that students gained knowledge of the self and others, increased their open-mindedness and acquired new reference frames. Students gained clear insights into personal ways of coping with intercultural situations. This self-knowledge and the awareness of one's learning process are considered essential for intercultural learning (Holmes and O'Neill 2012; Deardorff 2006). Finally, their overall understanding of the notion of culture changed towards a more non-essentialist view where culture is dynamic and identities are contextual and multifaceted (cf Holliday 2010).

This then delineates the second assumption, namely that intercultural ethnographies can serve as an important medium to make intercultural learning experience visible for students, teachers and possibly academics. Even though reflection reports offer only subjective descriptions and therefore selective views on reality (Deardorff 2015), the intercultural ethnographies demonstrate the learning outcomes of a mobility experience in terms of personal and intercultural growth. Upon return, the Intercultural Learning course offered students career training where they identified and verbalized their personal and intercultural growth in ways relevant to professional contexts. Therefore, future research could further investigate the use of ethnographies not only as a pedagogical instrument, but also as a method for formative assessment of intercultural learning.

## References

Agar, Michael. *Language Shock. Understanding the Culture of Conversation*. New York: William Morrow & Co. Inc, 1994.

Allport, Gordon W. *The Nature of Prejudice*. New York: Anchor Book, 1954.

Brewer, Elizabeth, and Jan Solberg. "Preparatory Courses for Students Going to Divergent Sites: Two Examples." In *Integrating Study Abroad into the Curriculum—Theory and Practice across the Disciplines*, edited by Elizabeth Brewer and Kiran Cunningham, 63–84. Herndon: Stylus Publishing, LLC, 2009.

Burns, Peter M., and Marina Novelli. *Tourism and Mobilities: Local-global Connections*. Wallingford: CABI, 2008.

Byram, Michael. *Teaching and Assessing Intercultural Communicative Competence*. Bristol: Multilingual Matters, 1997.

Deardorff, Darla K. "Identification and Assessment of Intercultural Competence as a Student Outcome of Internationalization." *Journal of Studies in International Education* 10, no. 3 (2006): 241–266.

Deardorff, Darla K. "In Search of Intercultural Competence." *International Educator* 13, no. 2 (2004): 13.

Dervin, Fred. "Cultural Identity, Representation and Othering." In *The Routledge Handbook of Language and Intercultural Communication*, edited by Jane Jackson, 181–194. Abingdon: Routledge, 2012.

Dervin, Fred. "Erasmus: 20 ans d'hypermobilité/hypomobilité existentielle?." In *Regards sur les mondes hypermodernes: Mythes et réalités*, edited by Fred Dervin and Aleksandra Ljalikova, 139–153. Paris: L'Harmattan, 2007a.

Dervin, Fred. "Mascaradesestudiantines finlandaises." *Les Langues Modernes* 1 (2007b): 27–44.

Dervin, Fred. *Métamorphoses Identitaires en Situation de Mobilité*. Turku: Turun Yliopisto, 2008.

Gaw, Kevin F. "Reverse Culture Shock in Students Returning from Overseas." *International Journal of Intercultural Relations* 24, no. 12 (2000): 83–104

Gullahorn, John T., and Jeanne E. Gullahorn. "An Extension of the U-curve Hypothesis." *Journal of Social Issues* 19, no. 3 (1963): 33–47.

Holmes, Prue, and Gillian O'Neill. "Developing and Evaluating Intercultural Competence: Ethnographies of Intercultural Encounters." *International Journal of Intercultural Relations* 36, no. 5 (2012): 707–718.

Hsieh, Hsiu-Fang, and Sarah E. Shannon. "Three Approaches to Qualitative Content Analysis." *Qualitative Health Research* 15, no. 9 (2005): 1277–1288.

ICEF. "Four Trends That Are Shaping the Future of Global Student Mobility." Monitor ICEF, 2015. http://monitor.icef.com/2015/09/four-trends-that-are-shaping-the-future-of-global-student-mobility/.

Jordan, Shirley Ann. "Ethnographic Encounters: The Processes of Cultural Translation." *Language and Intercultural Communication* 2, no. 2 (2002): 96–110.

Kim, Young Yun. "Intercultural Personhood: Globalization and a Way of Being." *International Journal of Intercultural Relations* 32, no. 4 (2008): 359–368.

Kim, Young Yun. *Becoming Intercultural: An Integrative Theory of Communication and Cross-Cultural Adaptation*. Thousand Oaks, CA: SAGE, 2001.

Kolb, David A. *Experiential Learning: Experience as the Source of Learning and Development*. Englewood Cliffs, NJ: Prentice Hall, 1984.

Kondracki, Nancy L., Nancy S. Wellman, and Daniel R. Amundson. "Content Analysis: Review of Methods and Their Applications in Nutrition Education." *Journal of Nutrition Education and Behavior* 34, no. 4 (2002): 224–230.

Krols, Yunsy, Joke Simons, and Gunilla de Graef. "Theoretisch kader. Interculurele competentie: een raamkader." In *Handboek Interculturele Competentie*. Brussels: Politeia, 2011.

Mayring, Philipp. "Qualitative Content Analysis." *Forum: Qualitative Social Research*, 2000. https://doi.org/10.17169/fqs-1.2.1089.

Messelink, H.E., Jan Van Maele, and Helen Spencer-Oatey. "Intercultural Competencies: What Students in Study and Placement Mobility Should Be Learning." *Intercultural Education* 26, no. 1 (2015): 62–72.

Mezirow, Jack. "Transformative Learning: Theory to Practice." *New Directions for Adult and Continuing Education* 74 (1997): 5–12.

Nazarkiewicz, Kirsten, and Gesa Krämer. *Handbuch Interkulturelles Coaching: Konzepte, Methoden, Kompetenzen kulturreflexiver Begleitung*. Göttingen: Vandenhoeck & Ruprecht, 2012.

Paige, R. Michael, and Michael Vande Berg. "Why Students Are and Are Not Learning Abroad." In *Student Learning Abroad: What Our students Are Learning, What They're Not, and What We Can Do about it*, edited by Michael Vande Berg, R. Michael Paige and Kris Hemming Lou: 29–58. Herndon: Stylus Publishing, LLC, 2012.

Passarelli, Angela M., and David A. Kolb. 2012. "Using experiential learning theory to promote student learning and development in programs of education abroad." In *Student learning abroad: What our students are learning, what they're not, and what we can do about it*, edited by Michael Vande Berg, R. Michael Paige and Kris Hemming Lou: 137–161. Herndon: Stylus Publishing, LLC, 2012.

Relyea, Clint, Faye K. Cocchiara, and Nareatha L. Studdard. "The Effect of Perceived Value in the Decision to Participate in Study Abroad Programs." *Journal of Teaching in International Business* 19, no. 4 (2008): 346–361.

Salisbury, Mark H., Brian P. An, and Ernest T. Pascarella. "The Effect of Study Abroad on Intercultural Competence among Undergraduate College Students." *Journal of Student Affairs Research and Practice* 50, no. 1 (2013): 1–20.

Spencer-Oatey, Helen, and Claudia Harsch. "The Critical Incident Technique." In

*Research Methods in Intercultural Communication: A Practical Guide*, edited by Zhu Hua, 223–238. Hoboken, NJ: Wiley Blackwell, 2016.

Spitzberg, Brian H., and Gabrielle Changnon. "Conceptualizing Intercultural Competence." In *The SAGE Handbook of Intercultural Competence*, edited by Darla K. Deardorff, 2–52. Thousand Oaks, CA: SAGE, 2009.

Thomas, Alexander. "Interkulturelle Handlungskompetenz-Schlüsselkompetenz für die moderne Arbeitswelt." *Arbeit* 15, no. 2 (2006): 114–125.

Trooboff, Stevan, and Michael Vande Berg. "Employer Attitudes toward Study Abroad." *Frontiers: The Interdisciplinary Journal of Study Abroad* 15 (2008): 17–33.

Untiedt, Jana. "Interkulturelle Erfahrung = Interkulturelle Kompetenz. Eine Untersuchung nach der sichtbaren Entwicklung interkultureller Kompetenz anhand von Reflexions-berichten des Kurses Intercultural Learning an der Universität Utrecht." Master thesis. Utrecht University, 2016.

Van 't Klooster, Erik, Jeroen van Wijk, Frank Go, and Johan van Rekom. "Educational Travel: The Overseas Internship." *Annals of Tourism Research* 35, no. 3 (2008): 690–711.

Van Maele, Jan, Basil Vassilicos, Lut Baten, Aminkeng Atabong, Luisa Bavieri, Ana Beaven, Claudia Borghetti et al. *IEREST. Intercultural education resources for Erasmus students and their teachers*. Annales University Press, 2015.

Vande Berg, Michael, Jeffrey Connor-Linton, and R. Michael Paige. "The Georgetown Consortium Project: Interventions for Student Learning Abroad." *Frontiers: The Interdisciplinary Journal of Study Abroad* 18 (2009): 1–75.

Vande Berg, Michael, R. Michael Paige, and Kris Hemming Lou. *Student Learning Abroad: What Our Students Are Learning, What They're Not, and What We Can Do About It*. Herndon: Stylus Publishing, LLC, 2012.

Witte, Arnd. "Reflexionen zu einer (inter) kulturellen Progression bei der Entwicklung interkultureller Kompetenz im Fremdsprachenlernprozess." In *Interkulturelle Kompetenz und fremdsprachliches Lernen: Modelle, Empirie, Evaluation*, edited by Adelheid Hu and Michael Byram, 49–66. Tübingen: Narr, 2009.

Zaidman, Nurit. "Stereotypes of International Managers: Content and Impact on Business Interactions." *Group & Organization Management* 25, no. 1 (2000): 45–66.

Zhu, Chen. "Contextualizing Generic Pedagogical Knowledge through Tension-focused Reflection: A Self-study." *Australian Journal of Teacher Education (Online)* 41, no. 6 (2016): 87.

Zhu, Hua. *Exploring Intercultural Communication: Language in Action*. London/New York: Routledge, 2013.

CHAPTER 19

# The Intercultural Deskpad: A Reflection Tool to Enhance Intercultural Competences

*Karen Schoutsen, Rosanne Severs and Jan D. ten Thije*

1       The Need for Intercultural Competence Development

Internationalization and diversity are vital to universities. While often driven by economic, academic and reputational factors, internationalization and diversity are also significant to universities' educational role and their role as employer, whether preparing university graduates for a globalized and diverse labor market, or creating a stimulating work environment for their staff to generate revealing knowledge. Yang (2002, 83) states that "internationalisation means the awareness and operation of interactions within and between cultures through its teaching, research and service functions, with the ultimate aim of achieving mutual understanding across cultural borders." Not only do international staff and students offer different perspectives, operation and interactions might also be influenced by other frames of references due to diverse backgrounds of the university's population. To strengthen Utrecht University's internationalization and diversity strategy by raising awareness and enabling staff to work effectively across cultures and with a diverse group of students or colleagues, a training 'Intercultural Awareness' was developed for non-teaching staff. This was done as part of the project 'Intercultural Competences for Utrecht University' (ICUU, that ran from 2017 to 2019) and is at the time of writing still part of Utrecht University's Human Resources development offerings.

This paper illustrates how a cyclical and non-essentialist approach to intercultural training contributes to the development of intercultural awareness and competences and underlines the importance of active and continuous reflection in this process. We will first elaborate on relevant concepts and theories, then describe the institutional context and case study at Utrecht University, and finish by delineating the rationale and usage of the *Intercultural Deskpad*, a reflection tool for Support and Administrative Staff to ensure continuous reflection and learning in pursuance of becoming interculturally aware and competent.

## 2 Intercultural Awareness and Competences

The definition of intercultural competence starts with a definition of culture. Recent definitions of culture acknowledge its multifaceted and non-static nature (Spencer-Oatey and Franklin 2009). For example, Spencer-Oatey (2008, 3) defines culture as a "fuzzy set of basic assumptions and values, orientations to life, beliefs, policies, procedures and behavioural conventions that are shared by a group of people, and that influence (but do not determine) each member's behaviour and his/her interpretation of the 'meaning' of other people's behaviour." In other words, culture might be a factor that impacts the frames of reference that people have to make sense of the world they live in and situations they encounter. This frame of reference guides people in what might become self-evident behavior in a given situation, and therefore might influence how one thinks, acts and communicates (Chen 1998). When different points of view, possibly influenced by culture, meet in interaction, this may lead to unexpected and puzzling situations, where one or neither of the interactants understand what is going on, how to behave or to interpret the interaction. Intercultural awareness can be seen as the cognitive perspective in intercultural competence (Triandis 1977) and provides individuals "with an opportunity to develop an understanding of cultural dynamics by reducing the level of situational ambiguity and uncertainty in intercultural interactions" (Chen 1998). Put differently, intercultural awareness assists in handling intercultural situations with more confidence.

Although intercultural competence can be defined in many different ways, many scholars agree that intercultural competences consist of a combination of attitudes, knowledge and skills (Deardorff 2006) enabling people to "communicate effectively and appropriately in intercultural situations" (Deardorff 2004, 194). In this definition appropriateness refers to avoiding violating valued rules and effectiveness to valued goals of the interactants (Spitzberg 1989). Besides the cognitive perspective, or intercultural awareness, according to Chen (1998) intercultural competence also comprises an affective aspect, namely intercultural sensitivity, and a behavioral aspect, or intercultural adroitness. In the final section we will explain how an educational method used in intercultural training can enhance intercultural awareness, as it is a crucial first step in developing intercultural skills, knowledge and attitudes. As Chen (1998) states "intercultural awareness functions as the minimum condition for interculturally competent individuals."

## 2.1 Developing Intercultural Competences

When developing an intercultural training, one can choose from many different models of intercultural competence development, either cyclical or linear. One well known model is the Development Model of Intercultural Sensitivity (DMIS), developed by Bennett (1986). The DMIS, introduced in 1986, investigates how individuals establish their identity by constructing boundaries of 'self' and 'other' within intercultural interactions (Bennett 2017). This is done by assessing people's behavior in intercultural settings and explaining how they interpret intercultural events. The DMIS model, and its adapted version the Intercultural Development Continuum (Hammer and Bennett 2012), distinguishes important stages in intercultural learning that evolve from ethnocentric stages or monocultural mindsets (i.e. denial, defense, minimization) to ethnorelative stages or intercultural mindsets (i.e. acceptance, adaptation, integration). This model offers a means for building intercultural competence, and training can contribute to moving onto further stages of development. However, moving progressively from one stage to another, such a linear set up may also imply that there is a final stage to being interculturally competent.

The Process Model of Deardorff (2006), which "creates a continuous process of working on attitudes, knowledge, internal outcomes and external outcomes related to intercultural competence" (Moeller and Nugent 2014, 4), on the other hand, is an example of a cyclical approach to intercultural competence development. According to the Council of Europe (2014, 17) an individual's intercultural competence is "never complete but can always be enriched still further from continuing experience of different kinds of intercultural encounter." This aligns with Deardorff's (2006) statement that competence development is a dynamic movement and a process from a personal to an interpersonal level.

In Deardorff's Process Model attitudes, knowledge and comprehension, skills, desired internal outcome and desired external outcome all relate to each other in different stages. Specific competences guiding one's attitude (willingness to be empathic, openness and respect towards other cultures, curiosity, tolerance of ambiguity, willingness to learn from and about people with other cultural orientations and engage in intercultural interactions), continue into the development of knowledge and comprehension (cultural self-awareness, deep cultural knowledge and sociolinguistic awareness) and may lead towards the development of skills such as listening, observing, evaluating and interpreting. These skills can also be described as the capacity of multiperspectivity, empathy (understanding and acting on opinions, values and emotions of others), cognitive flexibility (adjusting to a situation or context) and the ability to use all these traits in order to mediate between cultures (Council of

Europe 2014). From the personal level (of attitude, knowledge and comprehension, and skills), Deardorff's model moves to an interactive intercultural level, where the outcomes of one's intercultural competences are tested. Internal outcomes which lead to improved intercultural interactions represent the outcomes of an informed frame of reference, described as adaptability, flexibility and empathy (Deardorff 2006). This can be experienced as a challenge to one's attitudes, behavior and communication by people who have different cultural orientations to construct common views or perspectives (Council of Europe 2014). Lastly, the external outcome closes the circle in the circular process of developing intercultural competences with the ability to effectively and appropriately communicate and behave in intercultural situations (Deardorff 2006).

### 2.2 Working on Internal Outcomes by Experiential Learning

Deardorff (2006) emphasizes individuals' ability to reflect on their attitudes, skills and knowledge in order to accomplish an inner behavioral change in the form of internal outcome, the third stage in the circle. Nevertheless, the Process Model also shows that it is possible to reach effective and appropriate communication and behavior when omitting this third step. In other words, without internal outcome people can still have successful intercultural interactions. Yet, one could argue that this internal outcome is desirable and beneficial to the development of intercultural competences, as it supports people in consciously considering possible strategies when dealing with intercultural interactions, whether adapting to the other or being able to flexibly choose and use different communication styles and behavior in interactions, while taking into account contextual factors and the aim of the interaction. The Experiential Learning Model of Kolb (1984) aligns with this model, as it also focuses on a cyclical learning experience.

The experiential learning theory comprises four stages: concrete learning, reflective observation, abstract conceptualization, and active experimentation. Concrete learning happens when a learner gets a new experience, or interprets a past experience in a new way. This is followed by a reflective observation, where the learner reflects on the experience to attain understanding. Subsequently, abstract conceptualization takes place as the learner forms new ideas about abstract concepts or adjusts his or her thinking based on the experience and reflection on it. The fourth stage, active experimentation, is where the learner applies these new ideas, to see what happens if modifications in communication and behavior are made. This leads to a new concrete experience and so the cycle continues. Kolb (1984) argues that effective learning is realized as learners passes through all these different stages; however, influenced by learners' preferred learning styles, they can enter the cycle at any phase. The learning cycle can be completed over a short or longer period of time and can be passed through endlessly.

## 2.3  Moments of Wonder and Curiosity

Reflection, and maybe more specifically self-reflection, is essential when working on intercultural awareness and competences. As Boud et al. (2013) conclude, reflection is the key to turning experience into learning. The ability to reflect is, however, often a skill that participants need to be trained in. Knowing how to reflect, what questions need to be asked, let alone knowing how to learn from these reflections, cannot be taken as a self-evident and automatic process. Furthermore, the practice of reflection usually takes time and energy, also because, as Boud et al. (2013) affirm, feelings and emotions are involved, which represent both barriers *and* incentives. Thus, generally reflection needs to be guided, especially during a person's first conscious encounter with intercultural awareness and competences. Not only the ability to reflect is a skill that can be trained, the openness to reflection, in other words 'reflectiveness,' could also be seen as an attitude component of intercultural competence. Hoffman and Verdooren (2018, 71) describe reflectiveness as "the willingness to critically analyze and evaluate one's own thoughts and actions. To make fair judgments in intercultural interactions, one must be willing to consider how personal convictions, preferences, biases and habits influence one's judgment or actions." Reflectiveness is crucial to consider which approach or action to take in a given situation." This relates to Deardorff's (2006) statement that intercultural competence development all starts with attitude. Without a minimum degree of respect (valuing other cultures), openness (withholding judgment), curiosity; discovering (tolerating ambiguity) (Deardorff 2006) and empathy, inclusiveness, flexibility and reflectiveness (Hoffman and Verdooren 2018), the readiness to learn from experiences will probably be limited. As a result, an individual will not be able to pass through the different stages of Kolb's (1984) learning cycle.

Although individuals can enter the cycle in different phases, the Intercultural Awareness training described in the case study below tries to train participants in identifying concrete (intercultural) experiences to initiate their active reflection and learning. To this end, participants are introduced to the concept of 'rich points' (Agar 1994). Rich points are surprising experiences that deviate from participants' expectations: moments of wonder and curiosity that make them start comparing, analyzing and reflecting upon their own cultural background and that of the other. Rich points can be large and comprehensive, but can also be minor events. Questioning interpretations of behavior in these situations can lead to a more in-depth understanding of both differences and similarities in norms and customs. In other words, the 'Intercultural Awareness' training takes rich points as the starting point for developing intercultural competences.

### 2.4 Intercultural or Institutional?

Besides a cyclical approach on learning, focus on reflection and the use of 'rich points' as a central concept, in the training special attention is also paid to the analysis of institutional factors within these moments of wonder and curiosity. Often misunderstandings within intercultural communication are directly linked to differences in cultural frameworks, such as the cultural dimensions of Hofstede (1980; 2001) or dimensions in behavioral difference, such as high context-low context communication, monochronic-polychronic time and the use of personal space (Hall 1976). In order to trigger non-essentialist thinking about intercultural communication and to avoid the pitfall of the minimum object and the maximum interpretation (Koole and ten Thije 1994; 2001), i.e. perceiving culture as the main explanation for misunderstandings, the training differentiates between institutional communication, the way processes and communication are organized, and intercultural communication, the way in which linguistic diversity or cultural frames of references become relevant in interactions. As Koole and Ten Thije (2001, 573) state: "If we want to avoid this pitfall we have to ask ourselves the following question: how is our object of research related to the reality of which it is part?" This does not mean, however, that the institutional and intercultural perspective are entirely separate. Institutional elements can be seen as an expression of organizational culture. As Hoffman and Verdooren conclude (2018, 244), "the culture of a collective, a social group, can also be recognized by the way things are organized."

In the present case study, the focus on intercultural competence development as a cyclical and ongoing process, with an explicit role for active and continuous reflection, motivates our choice for combining Deardorff's Process Model (2006), the Experiential Learning Model by Kolb (1984) and the concept of 'rich points' (Agar 1994) as the main theoretical frame for the training. Furthermore, by including the Council of Europe's (2014) view on intercultural competence, which connects to a non-essentialist approach to intercultural communication, both internationalization and diversity perspectives are incorporated in Utrecht University's intercultural training.

## 3   Intercultural Training

Several researchers, among which Untiedt and Messelink (chapter 18) and Cole (chapter 15) in this book, argue that intercultural experience in itself does not necessarily lead to intercultural learning. Reflection and analysis is needed to facilitate this process (Alred, Byram and Fleming 2003; Jackson 2010) and intercultural training can provide this support. There are many types of intercultural trainings. The differences are not only caused by the different target groups (e.g. expats and their families about to go abroad, professionals, organizations, students or pupils that prepare themselves for an exchange abroad), although this may be decisive in some cases, but can also be linked to different approaches and aims of the training.

An important distinction needs to be made here between essentialist (culture-specific) and non-essentialist (culture-general) approaches in intercultural trainings (Gudykunst and Hammer 1983; Müller-Jacquier and ten Thije 2005; Porila and ten Thije 2008; Van Maele and Messelink 2019). Where culture-specific training focuses on cultural knowledge as the pathway to understanding the 'Other,' culture-general training focuses more on (cultural) awareness which, first of all, leads to a better understanding of the 'Self,' rather than of the 'Other.' This self-awareness facilitates participants' reflection on what comes natural to them in behavior and communication, which may be different for those with a different (cultural) background. In other words, awareness is the first step in being able to recognize self-evidencies, question them and subsequently analyze what norms, values, (cultural) frame of reference they are based on, and how they guide a person's actions and communication. The non-essentialist approach acknowledges the complexity of the world around us, of the 'Other' and the 'Self.' Instead of concentrating on a prediction of the other's behavior and providing participants with tools to deal with expected (often national culture-led) demeanor (i.e. dos and don'ts), however, the non-essentialist approach in intercultural training tries to facilitate the analysis of interactions, the questioning of interpretations and reflection on behavior. Yet this does not mean that the non-essentialist approach ignores the influence of national culture. Rather, it views national culture as only one viable influence on a person's cultural frame of reference which might affect interactions. The non-essentialist approach also takes into account other forms of (sub)cultures, e.g., cultures of social, religious and professional groups and communities of practice (Wenger 2000; Spencer-Oatey and Franklin 2009), which might influence a person's perspectives. Furthermore, it perceives culture, in its broadest form, as one of several possible factors influencing interactions. As Van Maele and Messelink (2019) conclude aptly on the difference between essentialist and non-essentialist trainings: "instead of teaching causal models that can attribute to predicting cultural behavior, a non-essentialist approach to intercultural training focuses on understanding when and how culture is made relevant by individuals themselves." In this way, a non-essentialist training leaves room for analyzing other factors, besides culture, that might influence behavior and communication, such as personal preferences and communication styles, previous experiences, (institutional) constellations or capacity, with the latter referring to participants' roles or positions in specific interactions.

The recognition of cultural, institutional and personal aspects in interaction enables the shift from focusing on adaptation, to the development of participants' own approaches in intercultural interactions. Although influenced by different (cultural and institutional) factors, participants should not ignore or overlook aspects that make them what they are and only focus on adaptation to the other in interaction. In the long run, this might not be a tenable and satisfying approach for the participant and overlooks the possible situation that the other interactant(s) might focus on adaptation as well. Hence, intercultural training with a non-essentialist approach concentrates on the development of necessary attitudes, skills and knowledge to deal with an infinite number of intercultural interactions with unpredictable individuals. Becoming aware of and building a repertoire of strategies is key in reaching this aim. Besides attitudes like openness, curiosity and respect, knowledge and comprehension, and skills, increasing awareness and applying effective intercultural strategies most of all requires flexibility, (occasionally) adaptability, an ethnorelative view and empathy, in other words, Deardorff's (2006) internal outcome. This emphasis on flexibility of strategies in communication and actions, rather than a mere focus on cultural knowledge and dos and don'ts (i.e. the essentialist approach), makes the development of intercultural awareness and competences even more important (the non-essentialist approach) (Porila and Ten Thije 2008).

## 4 Case-Study: Intercultural Awareness Training for Support and Administrative Staff in the Context of ICUU

According to the foreword of Utrecht University's Strategic Plan for 2016–2020, "The key challenges over the next few years will be to create an organization where staff are happy and successful in their work, and where students are able to realize their full potential" (Utrecht University 2016, 3). Utrecht University is an international research university, in the heart of the Netherlands, whose mission is: "Working together towards a better world" (Utrecht University, 2021). This mission translated into several goals for 2016–2020, among which creating a diverse and international community. Besides initiatives to attract a diverse and international student and staff population and to intensify the internationalization program, the Strategic Plan stated, "we will invest in intercultural skills for staff and students" (Utrecht University 2016, 26) to help students "to succeed in the highly globalized labor market" and teachers to "optimally cater to the international student body."

To realize these ambitions, in September 2017 the project Intercultural Competences for Utrecht University (ICUU, pronounced as *I see you*) started, led by Jan D. ten Thije. This two-year project was funded by the Utrecht Education Incentive Fund and was a cooperation between the Faculty of Humanities, Faculty of Science, Faculty of Law, Economics and Governance and University College Utrecht, and was supported by Utrecht University's Educational Consultancy & Professional Development department. Furthermore, the ICUU project installed an Advisory Board of about 40 members, which represented all other faculties and important stakeholders of Utrecht University, and a few key figures from outside the university. Every six months the ICUU project team would present the latest updates and discuss issues that had arisen with the Advisory Board. Through this group involvement, expertise on intercultural communication and competences that already existed within the university were exchanged and spread through all parts of the organization.

The focus of the ICUU project was enhancing intercultural competences of students and academic staff, as well as support and administrative staff. This translated into different aims per target group, namely (1) Visibility and accessibility of the intercultural course offerings for *students*; (2) Professionalization of *academic staff*; (3) Professionalization of *support and administrative staff* (SAS). Involving all institutional parties created mutual recognition in a common pursuit, enabling them to profit from each other's specific knowledge and skills. This shared approach turned out to be of key importance in realizing an inclusive and interculturally competent university community. So far, it seems a rather unique approach within Higher Education in Europe.

### 4.1    Training 'Intercultural Awareness for SAS'

'Intercultural Awareness for SAS' was developed as part of the ICUU project with the aim to assist Support and Administrative Staff in dealing appropriately, effectively and with confidence with a diverse group of students, colleagues and contacts outside of UU. In developing the training, a discourse analytical training concept was used (ten Thije 2001), with authentic video recordings of recurring communication situations of the target group of the training. These recordings were transcribed and then analyzed with regard to the concurrence of institutional and intercultural patterns (Lambertini and ten

Thije 2004; Porilla and ten Thije 2008; Cheung 2018). Subsequently, based on the authentic video recordings, role plays were created. These role plays represented the daily practice of the participants' workplace and created a framework to reflect upon all rich points participants wanted to share. After pilots at several International Offices and Student Service Desks, the final version of the training was offered for the first time in the Autumn 2018 as part of the official Human Resources training offer open to all Support and Administrative Staff at Utrecht University. At the time of writing, this is still the case.

While the training was initially developed and ran pilots for a homogeneous group of participants (i.e. International Office and Student Service Desk employees), the training that has been offered by Human Resources since the Autumn of 2018 is open to a very heterogeneous group, namely all non-teaching staff of Utrecht University, from communications and marketing advisors, policy makers and secretaries, to operational management, project coordinators and academic advisors. All Support and Administrative Staff (SAS) of Utrecht University who regularly encounter internationalization and diversity, e.g. through contacts with students, colleagues or contacts outside of the university, can sign up for the training. This challenged developers to make some modifications to the training in order to make it accessible, taking into account different types of prior knowledge, skills and experiences, and above all to make it attractive to a variety of positions within the university, with results and learning objectives that could be applied in various contexts. As Spencer-Oatey and Franklin (2009, 201) state: "the *general aim* of ICIC [intercultural interaction competence] development is to bring about change in the various components of an individual's ICIC, either by establishing them or by enhancing them." After four training sessions of three hours each, several assignments and meet-ups with a training buddy, participants should be able to work, to a greater or lesser extent, on all different *outcomes* of intercultural competence development, namely knowledge, skills and attitudes. The intended results of the training can be categorized in terms of these outcomes and linked to the affective, behavioral and cognitive components of intercultural competence (Spencer-Oatey and Franklin 2009).

The general aim of the Intercultural Awareness training is to develop intercultural awareness and competences, enabling participants to communicate (more) appropriately, effectively and with (more) confidence with a group of students, colleagues and contacts outside of Utrecht University. Table 19.1 shows a few examples of training activities connected to specific learning outcomes and competences. The next section will illustrate how the intended results and learning outcomes are embodied in the *Intercultural Deskpad* and how this tool is used in the Intercultural Awareness training.

TABLE 19.1  Overview of training activities linked to learning outcomes and intercultural competences

| Training activity | Learning outcome | Intercultural competence |
|---|---|---|
| Optical illusion image: discuss images that can be seen from different perspectives | Skills, attitude | Dealing with ambiguity, adjusting perspective |
| Presenting buddy activity: participants get to know each other by discussing the meaning of their names and have to present their buddy to the group | Skills | Active listening, openness |
| Exercise with steps DAE: describe, analyse, evaluate | Skills, attitude | Postponing judgment, adjusting perspective, reflectivity |
| Completing an identity map: who are you? | Knowledge, skills, attitude | Postponing judgment, cultural self-awareness, self-reflectiveness |
| Analyzing the institutional iceberg: discover different layers in communicative structures, based upon the Iceberg theory (Hall 1976) | Knowledge, skills | Cultural knowledge, cultural self-awareness, knowledge and critical understanding of the self |
| Discussing rich points | Skills, attitude | Analyzing, interpreting and relating, self-reflectiveness, listening and observing, empathy, postponing judgment, understanding of institutional and cultural factors |
| Role plays based on authentic video material | Skills | Active listening and observation, empathy, analyzing, interpreting and relating |
| Communication style activity | Knowledge, skills | Shifting perspective, active listening and observing, knowledge and critical understanding of language and communication |

## 5   A Tool for Continuous Reflection, Independently and with Colleagues

Zhu (2018, 167) states that "To achieve optimal intercultural learning through intercultural experience, it is essential to get the right balance between challenge and support." The challenge mentioned here concerns direct contact and experience (Kolb 1984). To make sure this balance is achieved in the Intercultural Awareness training, guidance in analysis, interpretation, reflection and learning (support) is offered to the participants by a tool: the *Intercultural Deskpad*, which represents an elaboration of the transfer approach. The aim of the *Intercultural Deskpad* is to help participants improve their intercultural awareness and competences by reflecting on moments of wonder and curiosity in their daily work that invite them to compare and analyze intercultural experiences, the influences of their cultural and institutional backgrounds and those of others, i.e. to capitalize on rich points.

The *Intercultural Deskpad* takes the shape of an actual deskpad in A2 size (42 by 59 centimeters). Each *Intercultural Deskpad* consists of 25 sheets. The English version is printed on one side of a sheet and a Dutch version on the other. In this way, the *Intercultural Deskpad* can be used by both Dutch and international staff members. Users are invited to place the deskpad on their desk under their keyboard. The idea is that, during office hours, they always see the deskpad lying on their desk and can therefore easily make notes about their rich points, as they occur in their daily work. During a break or in between meetings, they can carry out the analysis and reflection as it is pre-structured by the *Intercultural Deskpad*. When they have completely described and analyzed a rich point, they can tear off the page and can take it to a team meeting to discuss with colleagues. A digital version of the *Intercultural Deskpad* has also been developed, which users can fill out on their computers. They can print a page and bring it to their team meetings. During the Intercultural Awareness training, the participants receive a few sheets, analyze their rich points individually and then bring them to the training session to discuss the pages they filled out with the other participants and the trainers.

An unforeseen effect of using the deskpad outside of the training is that, because of its striking appearance with cheerful colors and symbols, a colleague with an *Intercultural Deskpad* on their desk signals an interest in intercultural communication. As a result, the deskpad could also give rise to conversations in the workplace with colleagues about everyday intercultural and institutional events. As the computer's keyboard is placed on the fields for writing down individual notes, these can be kept private if desired. This also offers a certain confidentiality to users' reflections. As the *Intercultural Deskpad* appears on desks in various departments, it also becomes clear that employees of Utrecht University are developing a common conceptual framework to talk about intercultural developments. In sum, the *Intercultural Deskpad* symbolizes a *Community of Practice* (Wegner 2000) aiming for shared intercultural competences and capacities.

## 5.1 Guided Awareness—The Intercultural Deskpad

The *Intercultural Deskpad* includes three different phases, where in phase two and three several constituents can be distinguished. Phase two and three also leave room for participants to write down *observations & insights* and state *points of interest/guiding topics & questions* that can support participants in their reflection. The tool integrates different models and theories in a logical structure, which will be reviewed below.

## 5.2 Three Steps to Intercultural Learning

In addition to the previously discussed *outcomes* (knowledge, skills, attitudes) and *components* of intercultural competence development (affective, behavioral, cognitive) (Spencer-Oatey and Franklin 2009), the *Intercultural Deskpad* uses the *components* as specific levels of reflection, including a fourth one, 'transfer' to facilitate structured and guided learning (C = cognitive level, A = affective level, B = behavioral level, T = transfer level, cf. Figure 2). These levels also correspond to the different aspects of intercultural competences, as discussed earlier by Chen (1998), namely intercultural awareness, intercultural sensitivity and intercultural androitness.

The three phases are to be followed in the order indicated by the arrows. This is to assist participants in considering different perspectives and interpretations of a situation, in other words stimulate openness. Furthermore, by guiding reflections and thoughts through the steps of Describing (phase 1), Analyzing/Interpreting (phase 2) and Evaluating (phase 3), the developers of the *Intercultural Deskpad* hope to (latently) encourage postponing judgment, and thus again openness. Finally, actions taken, based on the last two transfer (T) questions, could lead to phase 1 again, and therefore illustrate the cyclical approach of the tool itself. Besides stimulating the essential attitude of openness (phase 1–3), the *Intercultural Deskpad* also guides participants through reflections on their knowledge & comprehension (phase 2) and skills (phase 2–3) in intercultural interactions:

1. The *description* phase of the rich point: what happened? **(C)**
2. The *analysis & interpretation* phase of the rich point, including space to write down *observations & insights* **(C, A, B)**
   a. Institutional perspective: what happened at the institutional level? **(C, B)**
   b. Intercultural perspective: what happened at the intercultural level? **(C, A, B)**
3. The *reflect & learn* phase of the rich point: what can I learn from it? Including space to write down *observations & insights*. **(A, B, T)**
   a. Evaluation: how did I feel about it? What did I think of it? **(A)**
   b. What were my options for acting? **(B)**

c. What were my possible communication strategies? (B)
d. What would I do (differently) next time? (T)
e. Is this something to discuss within my team? (T)

## 5.3 Models and Concepts

The *Intercultural Deskpad* incorporates the theoretical models and concepts discussed in earlier sections of this paper to facilitate and support experiential and cyclical learning by using reflection on rich points and a non-essentialist approach to intercultural communication. Below we will explain how these models are embodied in the *Intercultural Deskpad*.

- Firstly, the non-essentialist approach to intercultural communication is represented by the definition and intercultural competence model of the Council of Europe (2014): in the intercultural perspective (phase 2) the jigsaw is a visual adaptation of the four-leaf clover of the Council of Europe. As can be seen, this model introduces a fourth *outcome* of intercultural competence development to the three *outcomes* identified in Deardorff's Process Model, one which Spencer-Oatey and Franklin (2009) place under 'attitudes,' namely 'values.'
- Secondly, the concept of 'rich points' (Agar 1994) occupies a central position in the *Intercultural Deskpad*. As the title and subtitle of the deskpad states the tool's objective is *Guided Awareness—An Intercultural Deskpad. Working on my intercultural competences and awareness: reflection on 'rich points.'*
- Thirdly, the experiential and cyclical learning process is incorporated by including Kolb's learning cycle. Although Kolb's cycle can only be found explicitly in phase 3, it is included in all 3 phases of the *Intercultural Deskpad*: the 'concrete experience' in this cycle equals participants' 'rich points' (phase 1). The stages of 'reflective observation' and 'abstract conceptualization' correspond to phase 2 and 'active experimentation' coincides with the transfer level of reflection in phase 3.
- Fourthly, in order to guide participants' analysis and interpretation (in phase 2) a distinction is made between institutional and intercultural factors.
- Lastly, although not visualized in the *Intercultural Deskpad*, Deardorff's Process model (2006) is essential in the deskpad's rationale. According to this model, even if the stage of *internal outcome* (informed frame of reference shift) is omitted, the *external outcome* (effective and appropriate communication & behavior in an intercultural situation) can still be the result. However, as we have indicated above and will substantiate in the final section of this paper, working consciously on intercultural competences is worthwhile and can be beneficial in both recurring and unexpected intercultural interactions. Consequently, the main focus of the training Intercultural Aware-

# THE INTERCULTURAL DESKPAD 155

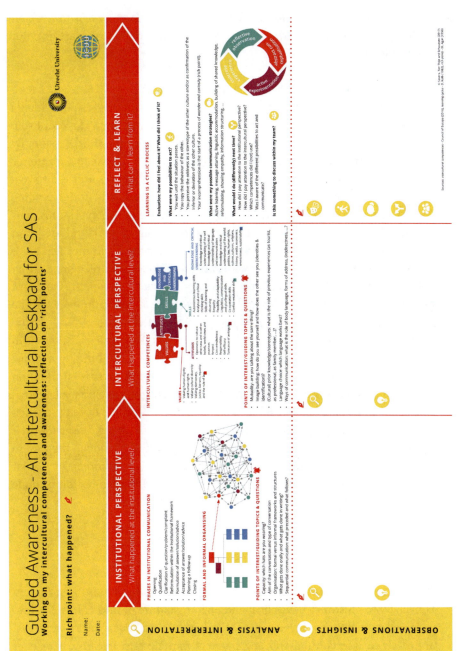

FIGURE 19.1   The *Intercultural Deskpad* and its three phases

ness for SAS, which is supported by the *Intercultural Deskpad*, is to work on Deardorff's so-called *internal outcome* by using rich points as a starting point for reflection.

### 5.4 Use of the Intercultural Deskpad

All different aspects of the *Intercultural Deskpad* are introduced to participants in sessions one to three of the training. To increase its effect, the tool itself, however, is only presented to participants at the end of the third session. By waiting until the end of session three participants should have, to a greater or lesser extent, developed an increased intercultural awareness and will have a better chance of seeing connections, recognizing elements and understanding and appreciating the use of the tool in their work. In between sessions, participants are encouraged to identify rich points while at work and are given exercises to guide their analysis of and reflection on these situations. This guidance builds up throughout the sessions, from the ability to recognize a rich point to a more step by step plan of reflection, so that participants can learn from their moments of wonder and curiosity. This process culminates in the guidance that the *Intercultural Deskpad* provides. After session three, participants are asked to work with the tool by exploring and analyzing rich points in a professional setting, and to discuss the outcomes with their buddy, a fellow participant. During the fourth and last session of the training, special attention is paid to practicing with the different phases within a specific professional setting and examining how the tool can be used to further develop participants' intercultural competences, either independently or together with their team. In this way we hope to stimulate participants to introduce the tool to their colleagues and include the usage of the tool as a component of regular team meetings, or stimulate (cultural) reflection amongst teams, for example through team intervision sessions.

## 6 Conclusions

This article has elaborated on a case study of an intercultural training at Utrecht University to illustrate the cyclical and ongoing nature of intercultural awareness and competence development. We have shown that a non-essentialist approach to intercultural training benefits participants, because it teaches them competences to act and communicate more effectively and with more confidence in an unpredictable, *superdiverse* (Vertovec 2007) and complex world, in which they encounter people with a variety of linguistic and cultural backgrounds. By offering participants a tool like the *Intercultural Deskpad* to analyze and learn from their 'rich points,' we hope to keep stimulating participants' continuous process of reflection, individually or with their team. Intercultural learning never ends and therefore an advanced training may create extra guidance for those who aim to develop specific intercultural competences, relevant for certain positions and work contexts, after having followed the basic training. Utrecht University's Human Resources has also acknowledged this potential demand, and the Spring of 2021 will see a training 'Advanced: Intercultural Competences.'

The assessment of intercultural awareness and competences has not been an integral part of the trainings so far. We realize that forms of self-assessment like using and analyzing case studies that include self-report instruments and pre-tests or post-tests are unsuitable for convincingly measuring intercultural competence development. We would therefore suggest exploring other possibilities for intercultural competence assessment. Many different and often excellent tools have been developed over the years, yet we have not found an instrument that covers all essential elements that we aim to address during our training. Future research on a model of intercultural competence assessment is needed to create a method specifically applicable to employees of educational institutions, taking into account intercultural and institutional factors and the cyclical and ongoing process of intercultural learning, for the innovative potential of the *Intercultural Deskpad* is clear: "With its cheerful colours, it is also a nice reminder for colleagues to see intercultural communication not as an individual problem, but as a collective learning process from which the university as a whole can benefit. These are the small steps by which intercultural changes are put into practice" (ten Thije 2020, 15).

### References

Agar, Michael. *Language Shock. Understanding the Culture of Conversation.* New York: William Morrow & Co. Inc, 1994.

Alred, Geof, Michael Byram, and Mike Fleming. *Intercultural Experience and Education.* Clevedon: Multilingual Matters, 2003.

Bennett, Milton J. "A Developmental Approach to Training for Intercultural Sensitivity." *International Journal of Intercultural Relations* 10, no. 2 (1986): 179–195.

Bennett, Milton J. "Developmental Model of Intercultural Sensitivity." In *The International Encyclopedia of Intercultural Communication*, edited by Young Yun Kim, 1–10. Hoboken, NJ: John Wiley & Sons, Inc., 2017.

Bennett, Milton J. "On Becoming a Global Soul." In *Developing Intercultural Competence and Transformation: Theory, Research and Application in International Education*, edited by Victor Savicki, 13–31. Sterling: Stylus, 2008.

Boud, David, Rosemary Keogh, and David Walker. *Reflection: Turning Experience into Learning*. London/New York: RoutledgeFalmer, 2013.

Chen, Guo-Ming, and William J. Starosta. "A Review of the Concept of Intercultural Awareness." *Human Communication* 2 (1998–1999): 27–54.

Cheung, A.T.U. "Intercultural Communication of the International Officers of Utrecht University. An Interaction Analysis of Conversations of International Officers with Local and International Students." Master thesis, Utrecht University, 2018.

Deardorff, Darla K. "Identification and Assessment of Intercultural Competence as a Student Outcome of Internationalization." *Journal of Studies in International Education* 10, no. 3 (2006): 241–266.

Deardorff, Darla K. "The Identification and Assessment of Intercultural Competence as a Student Outcome of International Education at Institutions of Higher Education in the United States." Dissertation, North Carolina State University, 2004.

"Developing Intercultural Competence through Education." In *Pestalozzi Series No. 3*, edited by Joseph Huber. Strasbourg: Council of Europe Publishing, 2014.

Gudykunst, William B., and Mitchell R. Hammer. "Basic Training Design: Approaches to Intercultural Training." In *Handbook of Intercultural Training: Issues in Theory and Design 1*, edited by Dan Landis and Richard W. Brislin, 118–154. Oxford: Pergamon Press, 1983.

Hall, Edward T. *Beyond culture*. Garden City, NY: Anchor, 1976.

Hammer, Mitchell R., and Milton Bennett. "The Intercultural Development Inventory." In *Student Learning Abroad: What Our Students Are Learning, What They're Not, and What We Can Do about It*, edited by Michael Vande Berg, R. Michael Paige and Kris Hemming Lou, 115–136. Herndon: Stylus Publishing, LLC, 2012.

Hoffman, Edwin, and Arjan Verdooren. *Diversity Competence. Cultures Don't Meet, People Do*. Bussum: Coutinho, 2018.

Hofstede, Geert. *Culture's Consequences: Comparing Values, Behaviors, Institutions and Organizations across Nations*. Thousand Oaks, CA: SAGE, 2001.

Jackson, Jane. *Intercultural Journeys: From Study to Residence Abroad*. New York: Palgrave Macmillan, 2010.

Kolb, David. *Experiential Learning: Experience as the Source of Learning and Development*. Englewood Cliffs, NJ: Prentice Hall, NJ, 1984.

Koole, Tom, and Jan D. ten Thije. "The Reconstruction of Intercultural Discourse: Methodological Considerations." *Journal of Pragmatics*, 33, no. 4 (2001): 571–587.

Koole, Tom, and Jan D. ten Thije. *The Construction of Intercultural Discourse. Team Discussions of Educational Advisers*. Amsterdam/Atlanta: RODOPI, 1994.

Lambertini, Lucia, and Jan D. ten Thije. "Die Vermittlung interkulturellen Handlungswissens mittels der Simulation authentischer Fälle." In *Analyse und Vermittlung von Gesprächskompetenz*, edited by Michael Becker-Mrotzek and Gisela Brünner, 175–199. Radolfzell: Lang: Verlag für Gesprächsforschung, 2004.

Messelink, H.E., Jan Van Maele, and Helen Spencer-Oatey. "Intercultural Competencies: What Students in Study and Placement Mobility Should Be Learning." *Intercultural Education* 26, no. 1 (2015): 62–72.

Moeller, Aleidine Kramer, and Kristen Nugent. "Building Intercultural Competence in the Language Classroom." In *Unlock the Gateway to Communication*, edited by Stephanie Dhonau, 1–18. Eau Claire, WI: Crown Prints, 2014.

Müller-Jacquier, Bernd, and Jan D. ten Thije. "Interkulturelle Kommunikation: interkulturelles Training und Mediation." In *Perspektiven interkultureller Mediation. Grundlagentexte zur kommunikationswissenschaftlichen Analyse triadischer Verständigung. Studien zur interkulturellen Mediation Bd. 2.*, edited by Dominic Busch and Hartmut Schröter, 367–382. Frankfurt am Main: Peter Lang, 2005.

Porila, Astrid, and Jan D. ten Thije. *Gesprächsfibel für interkulturelle Kommunikation in Behörden*. Berlin: Lang, 2008.

Spencer-Oatey, Helen, and Peter Franklin. *Intercultural Interaction: A Multidisciplinary Approach to Intercultural Communication*. New York: Palgrave Macmillan, 2009.

Spencer-Oatey, Helen. *Culturally Speaking. Culture, Communication and Politeness Theory*. London: Continuum, 2008.

Spitzberg, Brian H. "Issues in the Development of a Theory of Interpersonal Competence in the Intercultural Context." *International Journal of Intercultural Relations* 13, no. 3 (1989): 241–268.

Thije, Jan D. ten. "Ein diskursanalytisches Konzept zum interkulturellen Kommunikations-training." In *Im Netzwerk interkulturellen Handelns. Theoretische und praktischen Perspektiven der interkulturellen Kommunikationsforschung*, edited by Jürgen Bolten and Daniela Schröter, 177–204. Sternenfels: Verlag Wissenschaft & Praxis, 2001.

Thije, Jan D. ten. "Intercultural Communication as Mediation." Inaugural lecture given at Utrecht University, Utrecht, 2020.

Triandis, Harry C. "Theoretical Framework for Evaluation of Cross-cultural Training Effectiveness." *International Journal of Intercultural Relations* 1, no. 4 (1977): 19–45.

Utrecht University. "Mission and Vision." Utrecht University, accessed February 18, 2021. https://www.uu.nl/en/organisation/profile/mission-and-strategy.

Utrecht University. "Strategic Plan 2016–2020." Utrecht University, 2016. https://www.uu.nl/sites/default/files/ubd_strategic_plan_utrecht_university_2016-2020.pdf.

Van Maele, Jan, and Annelies Messelink. "Mobilizing Essentialist Frameworks in Non-essentialist Intercultural Training." In *Intercultural Foreign Language Teaching and Learning in Higher Education Contexts*, edited by Piotr Romanowski and Ewa Bandura, 141–161. Hershey, PA: IGI Global, 2019.

Vertovec, Steven. "Super-diversity and Its Implications." *Ethnic and Racial Studies* 30, no. 6 (2007): 1024–1054.

Wenger, Etienne. "Communities of Practice and Social Learning Systems." *Organization* 7, no. 2 (2000): 225–246.

Yang, Rui. "University Internationalisation: Its Meanings, Rationales and Implications." *Intercultural Education* 13, no. 1 (2002): 81–95.

Zhu, Hua. *Exploring Intercultural Communication: Language in Action*. Abingdon: Routledge, 2018.

APPENDIX

# Contents Volume 1

List of Figures and Tables   VII
Notes on Contributors   IX

1  Introduction: The Impact of (Non-)Essentialism on Defining Intercultural Communication   1
    *Jan D. ten Thije*

### PART 1
*Interactive Approach*

2  Discourse-Pragmatic Description   27
    *Kristin Bührig and Jan D. ten Thije*

3  It's Not All Black and White: Ethnic Self-Categorization of Multiethnic Dutch Millennials   69
    *Naomi Kok Luis*

4  Informal Interpreting in General Practice: Interpreters' Roles Related to Trust and Control   86
    *Rena Zendedel, Bas van den Putte, Julia van Weert, Maria van den Muijsenbergh and Barbara Schouten*

5  Gender Studies and Oral History Meet Intercultural Communication   104
    *Izabella Agárdi, Arla Gruda, Shu-Yi (Nina) Huang and Berteke Waaldijk*

### PART 2
*Contrastive Approach*

6  Cultural Filters in Persuasive Texts: A Contrastive Study of Dutch and Italian IKEA Catalogs   123
    *Jan D. ten Thije and Manuela Pinto*

7   An Analysis of Dutch and German Migration Discourses   136
     *Christoph Sauer*

**PART 3**
## *Cultural Representational Approach*

8   Cultural Representation in Disney's *Cinderella* and Its Live-Action Adaptation   155
     *Azra Alagić and Roselinde Supheert*

9   Turkish Transformations through Italian Eyes   169
     *Raniero Speelman*

10  Fading Romantic Archetypes: Representing Poland in Dutch National Press in 1990 and 2014   187
     *Emmeline Besamusca and Daria van Kolck (Boruta)*

    Appendix: Contents Volume 2   209
    Index of Names   211
    General Index   213

# Index of Names

Akker, Jan van den  114
Argyri, Froso  62
Augst, Gerhard  48

Bennett, Milton J.  143
Biber, Douglas  54
Blommaert, Jan  87
Bosma, Ulbe  6
Boud, David  145
Brewer, Elizabeth  125

Chen, Guo-Ming  142
Clark, Victoria  54
Cole, Debbie  115, 147
Connor-Linton, Jeffrey  124
Cornips, Leonie  62, 70
Coulmas, Florian  8
Cummins, Jim  43, 53

Deardorff, Darla K.  127, 143–145, 148, 154

Egger, Evelyn  62

Faigel, Peter  48
Feilke, Helmuth  48
Fhlannchadha, Siobhan Nic  61
Franklin, Peter  150, 154

Gülbeyaz, Esin Işil  52

Hewitt, Rosalind  22
Hickey, Tina M.  61
Hoffman, Edwin  145
Hofstede, Geert  146
Hulk, Aafke  62, 70

Kaltsa, Maria  62
Kim, Young Yun  127
Kolb, David  126, 130, 133, 136, 144, 154
Koole, Tom  146
Kuiper, Koenraad  23

Langendoen, Terence  86

Maas, Utz  43
Meadows, Brian  115
Messelink, Annelies  124, 147
Mezirow, Jack  127
Mills, Anne E.  61, 63

Paige, R. Michael  124
Pinget, Anne-France  9

Raben, Remco  6

Siekmeyer, Anne  54
Solberg, Jan  125
Spencer-Oatey, Helen  124, 142, 150, 154

Theuns, Dorien  9
Thije, Jan D. ten  146, 149
Tsimpli, Ianthi Maria  62

Untiedt, Jana  130, 147

Van Maele, Jan  124, 147
Vande Berg, Michael  124
Verdooren, Arjan  145

Willems, Wim  6

Yang, Rui  141

Zhu, Hua  151

# General Index

abstract conceptualization   126, 144
acceptance   16, 20, 25, 79, 143
active experimentation   144, 154
active listening   151
adaptation   43, 93, 108, 117, 121, 127, 135, 143, 148, 154
adjusting perspective   151
adverbial attributes   46
adverbial clause   51
Albanian   28–30, 32–39
alignment   116
ambiguous identities   26
assimilation   39
attribution   46
attributive clause   51
awareness   28, 33, 84, 85, 95, 98–100, 108, 125, 127, 129, 132, 134, 137, 141–143, 145, 147, 148, 150–154, 156, 157

Bahasa Indonesia   8
BICS-CALP differentiation   43
bidialectal children   62
bilingual(s)   3, 9, 42, 43, 49, 50, 53–56, 59, 60, 63, 64, 66–71, 94
bilingual advantage   59
bilingual bootstrapping   59
bilingual education   49, 53
bilingual mind   59, 60, 67, 70
bilingualism   28, 59
biological gender   60, 63
blocking   80
bootstrapping   59, 60, 70
Border Studies   118

capacities for semiotic behavior   88
case study   141, 145, 146, 156
categorical equality   88
category   6, 45, 51, 82, 83, 88, 89, 97, 116, 128
category formation   84
CHAT format   65
code-switching   10, 118, 122
communication   36, 37, 40, 44, 45, 79, 80, 84, 85, 87, 88, 90, 93, 99, 102, 104, 111, 113, 115, 120, 129, 133, 144, 146–149, 151, 152, 154, 157
communicative events   28

communicative setting   37
complete and distinct systems   85
complex sentence   42, 45–47, 53, 54, 56
compound sentence   42, 45, 47, 49, 53, 56
conative   85n4
conceptualization   128, 130, 131, 133, 136, 144, 154
concrete learning   144
content analysis   9, 10, 25, 128, 136
context-embedded   44
context of arrival   38, 39
context of departure   38
context-reduced   44
crises   124
critical discourse analysis   111, 114, 115, 118, 120
crosslinguistic   44
crosslinguistic influence   63, 64, 67–69, 71
cultural adjustment   125
cultural-specific knowledge   133
culture-general knowledge   133, 134, 136
culture shock   124
culture-specific training   147
cumulative exposure   71
curiosity   143, 145, 146, 148, 152, 156
curriculum development   112, 114
curriculum.nu   112, 113, 113n2, 114, 115, 120–122

deculturation   128, 135, 136
defense   143
denial   143
Development Model of Intercultural Sensitivity   143
diglossia   28
dilalia   28, 37
discourse analytical training concept   149
diversity   79, 93, 97, 99, 111, 113, 115–117, 122, 141, 146, 150
Dutch citizen   6
Dutch language   6, 25
Dutch subject   6
Dutch windows   79–82, 89, 90

early bilinguals   3, 9
educational design process   121

GENERAL INDEX

elite language  8
emotive  85n4
EMVT5.1  113n2
Enriching  103
Erasmus Programme  93
Essentialism  83
essentialist trap  115, 116
ethnocentric stages  143
ethnocentrism  96
ethnorelative stages  143
ethnorelativity  127
etic and emic approaches  79
evidence-based research  114
exchange programs  93
EXMARaLDA  44
expectation  35, 83, 84, 99n4, 120, 126, 127, 132, 136, 145
experience  28, 53, 71, 81, 85–87, 89, 90, 93, 95, 97, 100–103, 105, 124–132, 134–137, 143–145, 147, 151, 154
experiential learning  126–128, 136, 144
experiential learning cycle  128, 136
Experiential Learning Model  144, 146
experimentation  126, 128, 130, 131, 135, 136, 144, 154
exposure  63, 64, 68, 71, 95, 102

Facebook  36
family talk  89
feature of alikeness  84
feedback  94–104, 106–107, 116, 122, 127
first-language instruction  49
foreign Orientals  4
frame of reference  86–88
freedom of education  111
Friulian  29–31

generalizability  122
German  29, 42, 43, 43n1, 44, 45, 48–50, 52–56, 62, 95, 97, 104, 112, 122, 134
Gheg  28
grammatical gender  60–63, 70
group membership  26
Guided Awareness  153, 154

high context  146
higher education  7, 42, 79, 93, 94, 97, 100n5, 106, 108, 121
homesickness  124

ICIC [intercultural interaction competence]  150
identity  3, 5, 9, 10, 12, 14, 16, 19, 20, 22, 23, 25, 26, 38, 40, 79, 83, 97, 104, 107, 108, 111, 113, 114n3, 116, 118, 122, 124, 134, 143, 151
inclusive approach to English  113
inclusive multilingual modes  80
Indies people  5
indigenous people  4, 7, 11
*Indische mensen*  5
Indo-European Union  4
*Indo-Europeanen*  4
Indo-Europeans  4, 4n5, 7, 8
*Indo-Europeesch Verbond, IEV*  4
*Indo*  4–7, 11, 13, 16, 19, 20, 20n25, 21–23, 25
inference  83
informal domain  36, 37
*inlanders*  4
institutional  146, 153
institutional perspective  153
integration  32, 48, 52, 94, 97, 103, 124, 143
intercultural  28, 77, 79, 87, 96, 104, 124–128, 137, 141–143, 145–157
intercultural adroitness  142
intercultural awareness  141, 142, 145, 148–150, 152, 156
intercultural competence  124, 127, 142, 143, 145, 146, 150, 153, 154, 157
intercultural competence development  143, 145, 146, 150, 153, 154, 157
intercultural contact  124, 126, 127, 137
intercultural deskpad  141, 150, 152–157
intercultural education  125
intercultural ethnographies  124, 127
intercultural evolution  128, 135
intercultural growth  107, 127, 128, 137
intercultural learning  124, 125, 128, 137, 153
intercultural perspective  153
intercultural sensitivity  142, 153
intercultural training(s)  124, 137, 141–143, 146–148, 156
interculturally aware  141
interior monologue  36
international mobility  93
international students  93, 94, 101, 105–107, 129, 132, 133
internationalization  93, 124, 141, 146, 149, 150
internship abroad  129, 136

intra-disciplinary traditions 79
Irish Gaelic 119
Italian 28–30, 32–39, 60, 95, 112

*Koninklijk Nederlandsch-Indisch Leger* (KNIL) 6
*kumpulan* 22, 24

L1 30–32, 35, 36, 38, 39, 42, 43n1, 49, 53, 54, 63, 64, 66, 67, 69, 70
L2 32, 34, 36, 42, 43n1, 49, 53, 54, 63, 64, 66–68, 70, 71
label 83, 84, 88
language acquisition 34, 48, 53, 56, 99
language assistants 94–107
language diversity 28
language enhancement 43, 44, 48, 53
language maintenance 38, 40
language of instruction 7, 8, 13, 42, 49
language policy 7, 79, 80
language sanctuaries 23
language shift 38, 40
language status 26
learner-external 70, 71
level of complexity 42
level of essentializing 88
lingua franca 7, 93
linguistic advantages 59
linguistic anthropology 3, 80
linguistic behavior 31–34, 36–38, 40
linguistic choice 40
linguistic diversity 114
linguistic families 28
linguistics 79, 80, 87, 111, 114
local repertoire 29
logistic regression 66, 69
low context 146

Malay 7, 8, 8n18, 9, 12
Maniagese 30
matter of need 36
matter of will 36
metacognitive skills 95
metacultural awareness 105
metalingual 85n4
metalinguistic 105
metaphors 90
migration 20, 30, 32–34, 38, 39, 49
minimization 143

mistakes 10, 100, 106
misunderstanding 119
mobility experience 137
momentary equality 84
monochronic-polychronic time 146
monoglot ideology 97
multi-repertoirial 87
multilingualism 37, 42, 49, 112–114, 117, 120–122
MULTILIT project 43
mutual understanding 28, 120, 141

narratives 63–66, 68–70, 126
nationalist standard practices 80
native speaker 65, 94, 107
(near-)native proficiency 10
*Nederlands-Indië* 3, 17
nominalization 48
non-essentialist 79, 80, 85, 125, 134, 137, 141, 146–148, 154, 156
non-transparent gender systems 61
norm violations or deviations 43, 50, 55
noun-external cues 60
noun-internal cues 60
number-one mentality 134

objectification 115, 116
opaque 61, 82
orate and literate structures 43
orate structures 53, 56
orate to literate continuum 44
Other 147

parenthood 38
peer feedback 93–97, 99n4, 100, 101n6, 102–107
peer-feedback project 94, 95
personal space 146
phatic 85n4
plurilingualism 28
poetic 85n4
positive and negative transfer 71
positive transfer 59, 60, 62, 70
pre-university education 112
prescription 115
prestigious language 37
prior knowledge 83
process model 143, 144, 146, 154
pronominal gender 59

GENERAL INDEX

pronoun(s)   32, 37, 61 *passim*
pseudo-homogeneity   97

questionnaire   32 *passim*, 101

re-entry culture shock   124
reading skills   30
reciprocity   97
rediscovery of oneself   107
reference   61, 62, 67–70, 82n2, 85–87, 90, 119, 127, 131–135, 137, 142, 144, 147, 154
reflection   80, 100, 102, 103, 103n7, 116, 120, 125–133, 136, 137, 141, 144–147, 152–154, 156, 157
reflection reports   102, 103, 128, 131, 132, 137
reflection tool   141
reflectiveness   145
register differentiation   43
religious identity   39
rich points   107, 145, 146, 150–152, 154, 156, 157
Royal Dutch Academy of Sciences (KNAW)   112–113

segmentation   47
'self' and 'other'   143, 147
self-confidence   104
self-estimation   125
self-reflectiveness   151
semantic principles   61, 63, 70
sense of legitimacy   104
shared incompetence   97
simultaneous bilinguals   3, 9, 60, 63, 67, 68, 70
Skype conversations   37
SLO (*Stichting Leerplan Ontwikkeling*)   112
Slovenian   29
slower pace   59
social prestige   30, 37
Sometimes, but not always   88
speech community   3, 9, 10, 26, 30, 32, 34, 35, 38, 39

*Sprachausbau*   43
stereotypes   120, 128, 132
student mobility   93, 107, 124
study abroad   105, 124, 126
studying abroad   93
subject-verb-object   55
subordinate language   37
subordination   46–48, 53–56
superdiverse   156
superdiversity   79
*Symbolfeld*   45
syntactic complexity   43–45, 47, 48, 52, 55
syntactic development   50
system of reference   86

taalwijs.nu   120
teacher training   122
third-party verification   132
threading   80
tolerating ambiguity   145
Tosk   28
transformative learning   127
Turkish   42, 43n1, 44, 45, 48–50, 52–56, 112, 122
Turkish-German bilingual   42, 49, 50
Twitter   36
typological differences   53, 60

unification   30
'us' and 'them'   115

Venetian   28–31
verification through third parties   128
vicinity   39
vitality   31, 35, 38, 40
vocabularies   59
vocational education   112

written language acquisition   56
written language development   42, 45, 47, 49, 52, 53

Printed in the United States
by Baker & Taylor Publisher Services